The Nurse's Legal Advisor

The Nurse's Legal Advisor

YOUR GUIDE TO LEGALLY SAFE PRACTICE

J. B. LIPPINCOTT COMPANY
Philadelphia
London
Mexico City
New York
St. Louis
São Paulo
Sydney

ARNOLD S. GOLDSTEIN, JD, LLM
Professor, Health Care Law
Northeastern University
Boston, Massachusetts

SUE PERDEW, RN, PhD
Chairperson and Associate Professor
Department of Nursing
Marywood College
Scranton, Pennsylvania

SUSAN S. PRUITT, RN, PhD
Director of Treatment
Tarrant County Psychiatric Center
Tarrant County MHMR Services
Ft. Worth, Texas
Adjunct Faculty
School of Nursing
University of Texas at Arlington
Arlington, Texas

Acquisitions/Sponsoring Editor: Patricia L. Cleary
Interior Design: Russell H. Till
Cover Design: Jean S. Morley
Indexer: Irene Glynn
Compositor: The Composing Room of Michigan, Inc.
Printer/Binder: R. R. Donnelley & Sons Company

1 3 5 6 4 2

Library of Congress Cataloging-in-Publication Data

Goldstein, Arnold S.
The nurse's legal advisor / by Arnold S. Goldstein, Sue Perdew, Susan S. Pruitt.
p. cm.
Includes index.
ISBN 0-397-54700-5
1. Nurses—Malpractice—United States. 2. Nursing—Law and legislation—United States. I. Perdew, Sue. II. Pruitt, Susan S. III. Title.
[DNLM: 1. Ethics, Nursing. 2. Legislation, Nursing—United States. 3. Malpractice—United States—Legislation. WY 33 AA1 G6n]
KF2915.N83G65 1989
346.7303'32—dc19
[347.306332]
DGPO/DLC
for Library of Congress 88-12772

Any procedure or practice described in this book should be applied by the health-care practitioner under appropriate supervision in accordance with professional standards of care used with regard to the unique circumstances that apply in each practice situation. Care has been taken to confirm the accuracy of information presented and to describe generally accepted practices. However, the authors, editors, and publisher cannot accept any responsibility for errors or omissions or for consequences from application of the information in this book and make no warranty, express or implied, with respect to the contents of the book.

Preface

The possibility of liability affects every health care provider and it is no less a concern to today's nurse.

As an increasing trend, this possibility of liability has had a dramatic impact on how care is provided, the risks practitioners are willing to accept, and even the cost. It is that fear of the lawsuit, and the apparent willingness of more and more patients to file it, that requires all providers understand how malpractice claims arise, and then to take a long hard look at their own mode of practice with the objective of reducing liability, while providing the patient with the care he or she is entitled to.

"Liability" or "malpractice" are not problems of concern only to the medical profession. In reality the problem extends to every member of the health care team as they are all potential defendants once a malpractice claim arises. With ever-increasing frequency, other health professionals are being held accountable as targets of the patient turned plaintiff. And unquestionably nurses will have their actions evaluated with increased scrutiny.

That's what this book is designed to accomplish. It will be more than a presentation of the law. It will be an effective guide highlighting specific problems, procedures and even trends that can create nursing liability. The most important features of this book are the clear, concise, and practical steps you can take to reduce or avoid that liability. *The Nurse's Legal Advisor* indeed provides ready answers to the everyday legal questions nurses ask.

We assume you have little or no legal background. In fact, this may be your first "in-depth" exposure to the law of your profession. With this in mind, we present the legal principles in simplified, easy-to-understand language. Legal terminology is kept to an absolute minimum. To assist you with those few unavoidable legal terms within the text, we have included a comprehensive legal glossary to refer to.

Law can be confusing. To clarify it we have extensively used short case examples to illustrate the application of the law to a practice setting. These cases not only bring the law to life, but aid you in deciding how you might handle the same situation in your daily work. As you proceed through the book, you will find an increased ability to apply the abstract legal principles to the hundreds of situations you encounter in your work.

For this book to have its greatest value it has to provide you not only with the general theories applicable to all malpractice actions, but moreover it must give you the specific and precise guidance for conducting yourself within your profession. This book contains that careful blend of the general theory of liability with the practical "how to do it" information you will need.

You will find a discussion on all the contemporary problems of nursing care, including the expanded obligations mandated by recent court decisions, governmental regulations, and the development of new technology and procedures used in the field. As with the rapidly changing state of the arts–and law–affecting all health practitioners, the nurse must not only react to the present but also anticipate the future. As these changes bring about new responsibility they also present new legal issues. We hope this book will accurately predict those future trends and adequately forecast their legal implications.

Let us provide a caveat. Law, like medicine, deals in probabilities and seldom absolutes. Many questions defy a certain answer because providing that ultimate answer or decision is the function of the court. To render that decision may require more facts than can be provided in this or any other book. Furthermore, a legal outcome will depend somewhat on the applicable law within a particular state together with all the factual and subtle legal variables that make each case stand alone. This is what makes law so mystical to the layman and perhaps so fascinating to the lawyer.

Faced with a specific legal problem you must rely on the advice of your own counsel. Only he or she can intelligently assess all the facts, apply the laws of your state, and give you the guidance and protection you need. No book can serve as his or her substitute.

It is our hope that when you complete this book you will have a firm understanding of how liability arises—where you may encounter it—and how you can avoid it. With that newly gained perspective you will be able to do what you were meant to do: provide the best possible nursing care.

Contents

1

Licensure and Practice Standards

As a nurse, you need a thorough understanding of how the practice of nursing relates to the law—the body of principles, rules, and regulations that govern your specific obligations toward your patient, your employer, and other health providers with whom you work.

In this chapter we answer important questions concerning these laws, how they relate to your practice and how they relate to one another. We specifically focus on issues relating to licensing because licensing laws and the nurse practice acts are largely responsible for defining the scope of nursing responsibility.

Nurses, like other health professionals, must be licensed to practice their profession. Governmental licensing is meant to protect the public and foster professionalism. The fact that licensing is a matter of state law, however, means that there is no uniform system. There are many different laws and regulations concerning both initial licensing and discipline of nurses. Despite this, there are a number of generally applicable legal considerations.

How is nursing practice defined?

Attempts to define nursing practice, through state statutes and suggestions propounded by the American

Nurses' Association (ANA), have not always been clear or successful. State nurse practice acts may be classified as either traditional or modern. Traditional statutes draw on the model definitions of "professional nurse" (i.e., registered nurse) and "practical nurse," as advocated by the ANA in 1973. The registered nurse (RN), as traditionally referred to, is educated in the biological, physical, and social sciences and in nursing skills; functions to observe patients and carry out treatments authorized by physicians; and, as a result, cares for the sick, aids in the prevention of disease, and conserves health. The education, function, and activities of licensed practical nurses (LPNs) are defined in a similar, but more elementary, manner. More modern nurse practice acts and the recently amended ANA definitions, in contrast, define nursing very broadly so as to allow for the advancement and expansion of the practice into other areas of health care. Most state laws, however, specifically prohibit nurses from practicing medicine, and attempts to define nursing are often nothing more than efforts to delineate the respective rights and responsibilities of doctors and nurses.

What provisions are typically found within state nurse practice acts?

While specific provisions vary from state to state, most practice acts include the following:

1. The definition of important terms including the definition of nursing and the various types of nurses recognized
2. A statement of the educational and other training or requirements for licensure and reciprocity
3. A statement as to permitted nursing practices

and/or acts (e.g., medical diagnosis) that may *not* be performed by a nurse
4. Conditions under which a nurse's license may be suspended or revoked
5. The general authority and powers of the state licensing agency having jurisdiction over nurses

Obviously, the state's nurse practice act is the most important law for every nurse to understand fully before entering practice.

How effectively do nurse practice acts define permitted nursing practices?

Although this depends on the specific state law, the trend is toward self-governance by the health professionals in hospitals; therefore, nurse practice acts have deliberately left to hospitals the right to define the scope of nursing responsibilities. For example, interdisciplinary committees consisting of physicians, nurses, pharmacists, and administrators may issue a joint statement defining permitted nursing practices within their facility. For this reason, some joint statements allow nurses to perform cardiopulmonary resuscitation (CPR), cardiac defibrillation, and venipunctures, whereas other institutions are more restrictive. Of course, joint statements do not have the force of law and are suggestive only of nursing responsibility to the extent otherwise not prohibited by law.

Do nurse practice acts state my specific obligations as a nurse?

Statutes that define and prescribe the areas of control of professional and practical nursing are usually drawn in broad, general terms and therefore do not provide precise legal guidelines for permitted conduct. The same can be said of statements of functions issued by nursing organizations. The courts have closed many of the gaps by applying general legal principles to the most commonly encountered situations. In this manner, the law of malpractice has been largely developed by the courts as a part of the common law.

As a nurse, what should I do if I am unsure about the proper interpretation of a nurse practice act?

Many nurse practice acts fail to define precisely a nurse's responsibility, leaving the law open to varying interpretations.

If you are in doubt about the proper interpretation of any law, you may request an opinion from the legal counsel for the hospital or perhaps legal counsel for the state nursing association.

You can also ask the state nursing board for interpretive guidelines, and frequently the state attorney general will, on request, issue an opinion.

It is critically important for you to understand your duties, particularly where your responsibilities start and end.

If a state statute and a state regulation are in conflict, which takes precedence?

Statutory law created by the legislature takes precedence over a regulation enacted by a licensing or administrative agency. Where the regulation is only stricter than the statutory law, then the laws are not in conflict with one another, and both the regulatory and the statutory law must be observed.

Similarly, federal statutes and regulations take precedence over state laws and regulations when a conflict exists. Here, however, it is more common to find only a permissibly stricter state law obligating a nurse to obey both the state and federal provisions.

What is not always understood is that federal regulations take precedence over state statutes. Federal regulations are generally more lenient than state laws, however, and you typically will follow the stricter state laws.

What should I do if I am unclear about a particular legal issue or interpretation of the law?

The safest practice is for you to request an interpretive guideline from the state nursing board. This is particularly true if it involves a regulation promulgated by the board.

An interpretation of a state statute may be obtained on request to the state's attorney general; he will then issue an opinion binding on the state.

When the issue involves hospital policy or procedure, you may also request an opinion from the hospital's legal counsel after consultation with appropriate supervisors and administrators. You certainly have the right to seek an independent legal opinion whenever you remain unclear about your responsibilities. Your attempts to obtain such an opinion clearly evidence a "good faith" effort to comply with the law, which would be important in any resultant disciplinary proceeding.

Should I consider nursing regulations to be enforceable laws or only recommended guidelines for proper practice?

Nursing practice regulations are generally established by state nursing boards. Regulations, of course, are always enforceable. Unless they are specifically cited as regulations (or state statutes), however, professional standards and codes of ethics are not laws and cannot be enforced as such.

As a nurse, must I consider the ANA's Code for Nurses legally binding on me?

No. You cannot lose your license specifically because you violated the ANA's Code for Nurses. As with ethical codes from other professional organizations, the ANA's Code for Nurses does not have standing as enforceable law.

Nevertheless, the ANA's Code for Nurses can be cited as a guideline of professional standards in a civil case. And, of course. many states have regulations that coincide with the ANA's code.

What authority do I have as a nurse practitioner in treating patients?

Your activities are based on protocols developed jointly by a physician and a nurse practitioner. Nevertheless, it may be argued that you are making what has traditionally been considered a medical diagnosis. This is why nurse practitioners are often in the center of the controversy surrounding nursing practice and diagnosis. Registered nurses may make diagnoses only in limited situations. Nurse practitioners regularly make independent decisions, in collaboration with a physician.

This authority derives from the relevant sections of the nurse practice acts. These are of two types. Some statutes provide for the regulation of the nurse practitioner by state licensing boards, which promulgate rules and regulations pertinent to the newly expanded role. Others allow traditionally medical functions to be delegated to the nurse practitioner on the grounds that the delegation was approved by the nursing and medical boards. Federal guidelines on reimbursement for certain activities by the nurse practitioner are of the latter type.

What qualifications must I have to become a nurse practitioner?

Since certification requirements vary, the ANA has attempted to establish national standards. As qualifications are still set by each state, however, requirements differ. The most common eligibility requirements include the following:

- Current professional nurse registration
- Bachelor of Science degree in nursing
- Statement of specialty practice area
- Two or more years of nursing experience
- Educational requirements set by the state nursing board (graduation from a practitioner program)

If you are interested in pursuing nurse practitioner status, you should check with the ANA or your state's nursing board for the specific requirements in your state.

As a registered nurse, can I legally assume the expanded role of a nurse practitioner in states where nurse practitioners are not recognized?

In states that do not yet license nurse practitioners, a physician (or hospital) cannot legally delegate to a nurse authority that goes beyond what a nurse may permissibly do under the state's nurse practice act. Therefore, if you accept such broad responsibility, you incur far greater risk of liability, which may include criminal or administrative sanctions, or both.

How is the composition of a state nursing board determined?

State statutes enacted by the legislature determine the composition and powers of the state licensing board and the procedure for selecting members.

Most licensing boards are composed primarily of nurses, although a sizable number of states also have physicians, consumer representatives, and hospital administrators on the board. In virtually every state, board members are appointed by the governor, often from recommendations submitted by consumer groups.

It should be noted that some states have separate licensing boards for RNs and LPNs, and the composition of these boards necessarily differs.

What procedures must a nursing board follow in a disciplinary case?

A licensing board is a public administrative agency, and as such, its procedures must satisfy the constitutional requirements of due process. The licensing board must also adhere strictly to its own rules and procedures. It may not alter them for some applicants and not for others.

The basic procedures for disciplinary action are nearly identical in all states. Often these procedures are set forth in the state's administrative procedure act and incorporated in the professional practice act. Disciplinary procedures provide that a licensee charged with unprofessional behavior be given sufficient notice of the charges and an opportunity for a hearing before any final disciplinary action is taken.

As a licensed nurse, you have the right to be represented by counsel, to present and cross-examine witnesses, and to present evidence on your own behalf. Since you have the right to judicial appeal of a final decision, the licensing board is required to keep an accurate and adequate record of the proceedings to serve as the basis for appeal.

Is a nursing board's final decision on a disciplinary proceeding subject to appeal?

You always have the right to appeal an adverse decision by a licensing agency. The grounds and procedures for appeal are found in the state's administrative practices act. The most common grounds for appeal are either that there was insufficient evidence to support the board's finding of wrongdoing or that the board violated constitutional or state-mandated procedures in the conduct of the hearing.

The courts seldom overturn a board's decision unless there has been a clear abuse of its broad discretionary powers, or the board otherwise violated a procedural rule designed to protect the nurse. On matters of professional judgment, however, the courts almost always defer to the board, both as to the findings and the sanctions imposed.

May I refuse to testify at my disciplinary proceeding?

Since a disciplinary proceeding is considered a civil proceeding rather than a criminal proceeding, you have no right to invoke the Fifth Amendment constitutional right against self-incrimination. Although a licensing board cannot compel you to testify, the board can accept a refusal to testify as evidence of liability or wrongdoing, an inference that cannot be drawn in a criminal proceeding.

What may a court do if it disagrees with the decision of a nurse licensing board?

The court can either reverse (or modify) the board's decision or remand the case to the board to be heard again. In many states, the court can hear and decide the complete case against the nurse. This is called a *trial de novo*.

Of course, if the licensing board disagrees with a lower-court ruling, the board has the right (as does the nurse) to seek a review from a higher or appellate court.

As a nurse, am I required to report a colleague's incompetence?

The American Nurses' Association says that "a nurse has a professional responsibility to safeguard the public when healthcare and safety are affected by the incompetent, unethical or illegal practice of any person." The Canadian Nurses' Association has a similar provision.

Although these are only professional codes and are not enforceable laws, professional codes can establish a standard of care.

In some states, the nurse practice act or the regulations of the state nursing board stipulate that a nurse *must* report improper, inadequate, or unlawful conduct. This trend is increasing.

Can I incur liability for reporting a nurse or other medical professional to a licensing board?

Not unless it can be shown that your complaint was made in bad faith and with the malicious intent to cause problems for the reported person. In such circumstances, the person complained of may bring a malicious prosecution claim.

If your complaint was made in good faith, however, you are generally protected from reprisal.

What risks do I run if I cover up a colleague's error or improper action?

It is always difficult to report wrongful conduct by a colleague, but failure to do so may create personal liability.

In some states, failing to report a nursing colleague's unacceptable conduct may be considered unprofessional conduct and grounds for disciplinary action. Then, too, the cover-up may lead to further harm to patients. If the cover-up involves a violation of law, the cover-up may make you an accessory to the fact and therefore criminally liable. Finally, not disclosing the problem may cause the colleague to defer getting help, for example, if drug abuse is involved.

What procedures should I follow to obtain a new license when I move to a different state?

When moving to another state to practice nursing, you must obtain a license of temporary practice for that state before legally practicing there.

You should contact the nursing board in the state in which you seek a license. The board will issue a temporary permit to practice for several months until your license application is processed.

The qualifications for licensure are reasonably uniform between states; therefore, nurses may move freely to new jobs in other states. Still, a state has the right to refuse reciprocity if you did not match the state's requirements at the time of your original licensure.

If I accompany a patient from one state to another, must I have a nursing license from both states?

No. Under such circumstances, the license to practice in one state is valid in all other states for the duration of patient-accompanied travel.

Similarly, if you are a nurse in the armed forces, you are required by federal law to hold a valid state license, but not necessarily from the state in which you are currently practicing.

What should I do if I inadvertently allow my nursing license to expire?

Several important steps should be taken. First, you should notify your supervisor. You should then notify the licensing board and request temporary or interim permission to continue practice. Finally, you should refrain from further practice until a new license or interim permission to practice is granted.

Continued practice without a valid license can be grounds for disciplinary action and may disqualify you from malpractice insurance coverage.

How difficult would it be for me as an American nurse to obtain licensure in a foreign country?

If you move to a foreign country, your U.S. license will be reviewed by the appropriate authority, which may accept it, reject it, or accept it subject to conditions. Most commonly, foreign countries (non-English-speaking) require nurses to complete a language-proficiency examination.

Reciprocally, many states are beginning to require that foreign nurses take and pass the examination prepared by the Commission on Graduates of Foreign Nursing Schools (CGFN examination) or pass the National Council Licensure Examination (NCLEX).

Under what conditions can my nursing license be suspended or revoked?

Your nursing license may be revoked or suspended for "good cause" as defined in the nurse practice act or other licensing statutes in a particular state, which are usually available from the state nursing board.

Common grounds for suspension or revocation include inability to function properly because of drug or alcohol addiction, lack of mental competency, or violation of the nurse practice act or other laws related to nursing practice. Some states include conviction on any felony charge as grounds for suspension; very few states suspend a license as a result of malpractice alone.

If my license is revoked, does this mean I can never regain my license?

Not necessarily. Frequently, a licensing board will reinstate a nurse's license after a sufficient length of time, provided the board is satisfied that the nurse is not likely to be a repeat offender.

You should petition the board for reinstatement. The board will base its decision on the severity of your original violation, the time lapse, and, particularly, evidence of your current fitness to practice.

2

Patient Rights and Hospital Policy

Like all nurses, you face issues involving patients' rights every day. How you respond depends partly on the legal responsibilities defined by your state's nurse practice acts. But it also depends on policies set by the institution where you work and, perhaps most important, on your understanding of the basic rights that belong to every patient.

Issues concerning a patient's rights are becoming increasingly important in nursing practice. First, hospital accreditation standards both recognize and enforce patients' rights, and so a violation of these rights may cause loss of hospital accreditation. Second, patients' rights are often nothing more than an explicit restatement of legal rights that otherwise exist. Therefore, their violation can create civil or even criminal liability.

A patient's bill of rights defines a person's rights while he is receiving health care. It helps protect these human rights at a time when the person is most vulnerable. Generally, patients' rights extend to such issues as human dignity, privacy, confidentiality, informed consent, and refusal of treatment. Patients' rights may even extend to rights to treatment, discharge, and explanations about medical costs.

Later chapters explore each of these rights in greater depth, but this chapter helps you understand basic responsibilities toward a patient in the context of general hospital policy and accreditation standards.

What standards must a hospital observe in order to receive Joint Commission for Accreditation of Hospitals (JCAH) accreditation?

The JCAH sets voluntary standards of operation for hospitals and other health-care institutions, and accredits those that meet their standards. To receive JCAH accreditation, a hospital must, as a minimum, do the following:

- Maintain a safe, clean facility and exercise continuous infection control.
- Publish rules and regulations for the medical staff.
- Publish the procedures physicians can follow to apply for medical staff memberships.
- Establish medical staff committees to review the quality of medical care given by its members.

Are the standards of the JCAH legally binding on hospitals?

Compliance with the JCAH standards is essential for continued accreditation and is important to virtually every hospital.

In some states, the JCAH standards of care have been specifically incorporated into state law; in these instances, the JCAH standards have become the statutory or regulatory standards that must be followed as operative law.

Even when state law does not refer to the JCAH standards, a court may rely on these standards as a measure of the applicable national standard of care to be observed by hospitals and health practitioners.

How often should I review hospital policy and nursing service policy?

Many risk managers suggest that you review these policies at least once a year. Considering the rapidity of change, however, it is wiser to review hospital and departmental policy thoroughly twice a year.

Whenever possible, you would also be wise to compare the policies in your hospital with the policies of other hospitals in order to discover possible new and improved methods for providing nursing care.

Is a hospital obligated to maintain written policies?

Yes. Every hospital and health-care institution must establish policies, that is, a set of general principles by which it offers health-care services. Moreover, the hospital must have reasonably delineated procedures for carrying out these policies. Courts have often held hospitals liable for poorly formulated or poorly implemented policy on health-care matters.

Many hospital policies and procedures are, of course, mandated by state or federal laws, such as Medicare and Medicaid, or through accreditation requirements. It would be difficult to find a hospital without some form of policy statement, although many hospital policies remain inadequate.

Are hospitals required to maintain policy-and-procedure manuals?

Yes. Hospital licensing laws in every state require each hospital in the state to establish policies and procedures for its operation.

It is usually the responsibility of the nursing service department to develop policies and procedures for nursing practices in the hospital, which then become part of the overall manual.

Staff nurses should insist on participating in policy decisions that have an impact on their practice and therefore on their legal responsibility.

How can I change or improve hospital policy?

One way to bring your suggestions to the attention of decision makers is for you to discuss policy problems at committee meetings and interdepartmental meetings. You may also propose policy changes directly to the hospital administrator through unit management committees, grievance procedures, and attitude questionnaires.

Is hospital policy considered law?

No. Nevertheless, many hospital policies are based on applicable laws or regulations. Further, the policy may reflect the operative standard of care for nursing practice and would then help define whether a nurse was negligent.

What should I do if hospital policy is in conflict with a law?

You must observe laws and regulations if they are in conflict with hospital policies.

You should, however, tell your nursing supervisor, hospital administration, or both about any conflict or discrepancy between hospital policy and the law. Such notification should then be included in the personal journal in which you date and sign entries.

Can a hospital's policy-and-procedure manual expand what is permitted under state or federal law?

No. Permitted practices under a policy-and-procedure manual may be narrower or stricter than what is allowed by state (or federal) law, but they cannot relax laws or otherwise condone practices that are not permitted by law. For this reason, it is particularly important to review your hospital's policy manual after any revision of state law.

How important is it for me to review a hospital's policies and procedures before I accept employment as a hospital nurse?

It's an excellent idea. Unless you feel reasonably comfortable with a hospital's operating philosophy, objectives, and rules, you will not feel comfortable with the job or the quality of care the hospital provides. If a hospital's policies are in conflict with your personal standards, you should look elsewhere for employment.

What items should I expect to be included in a nursing department manual?

Although there is no standard format, a reasonably complete manual should:

1. Define the limits of nursing action and practice (in conformity with the state's nurse practice act).
2. State how general hospital policies relate to the nursing department.
3. Offer guidelines for handling emergencies and incidents.
4. Provide standing orders for nurses working in certain areas, such as intensive care units (ICUs) or coronary care units (CCUs).
5. Disclose the nursing department's responsibility and role in the context of the overall institution.

Of greatest importance, the hospital must ascertain that these policies are consistent with federal and state laws and regulations.

How often should a nursing department manual be reviewed and revised?

A good nursing department manual will constantly be in the process of revision.

A complete review certainly is indicated when the hospital or other key department changes its policies, when new state laws or regulations are enacted, or when new JCAH guidelines and recommendations are to be implemented. The manual itself should include a requirement of periodic review, with review times designated by the appropriate committee.

What is meant by a patient's bill of rights?

A patient's bill of rights defines a person's rights in connection with the health care he receives. It helps protect the most basic rights due every patient.

In large measure, a patient's bill of rights merely restates the basic human rights recognized by courts; therefore, a patient has these same rights even without the adoption of a formal bill of rights by an institution.

Generally, a patient's bill of rights is designed to protect such basic rights as human dignity, privacy, refusal of treatment, informed consent, confidentiality, and disclosure of information.

Is a patient's bill of rights legally binding or enforceable?

Ordinarily, yes. Bills of rights that have become laws or state regulations obviously provide recourse to a patient whose rights have been violated. In certain instances, courts have held a patient's bill of rights to be part of a legally binding contract between hospital and patient, and therefore legally binding.

Bills of rights adopted by associations and accrediting agencies (e.g., the JCAH) are not legally enforceable but, if violated, can cause a hospital to lose Medicare and Medicaid participation and other governmental support.

To what extent must I comply with an institution's bill of rights?

A patient's bill of rights is legally binding on nurses. If the hospital where you work adopts a bill of rights, you are required to uphold those **rights**. Similarly, you must uphold the bill of rights published by the National League for Nursing (NLN).

Violation of these bills of rights can be evidence of negligent conduct and may expose you to disciplinary action by nursing boards if patients' rights parallel state law.

You have the responsibility to become thoroughly familiar with the hospital's bill of rights and with patients' rights mandated by state law.

What is a patient's right to health-care information?

Both common-law decisions and statutory provisions emphasize a patient's right to adequate information about his condition and treatment. Many hospitals specifically include this in their patients' bills of rights. The doctrine of informed consent further supports a patient's right to know.

Does a mentally incompetent patient have the same legal rights as a competent patient?

A patient's rights cannot be limited or denied solely because he is mentally ill or developmentally disabled. For example, a mentally incompetent patient ordinarily cannot be detained in a hospital against his consent, nor denied the right to refuse treatment or receive information needed for informed consent.

Under what circumstances can a mentally ill or developmentally disabled person be kept in a hospital involuntarily?

Such patients can be restrained from leaving a hospital if they are at risk of endangering their own lives or pose a threat to the property or life of another person.

The general test is this: If a patient is capable of surviving safely in freedom, by himself or with the help of willing and responsible family or friends, forced hospitalization is inappropriate and will not be sanctioned.

Restraint should never be used for the convenience of the institution, for punishment, or as a substitute for treatment programs.

What is meant by *habeus corpus*, and how is it used in unlawful restraint cases?

A writ of *habeus corpus* issued by a court literally means "deliver up the body." In the context of unlawful restraint, it would mean to release or free the patient.

If a court determines a hospital (or any other institution) is unlawfully and without justification holding a patient against his will, it will, on application brought on behalf of the patient, issue a writ of *habeus corpus*, which then compels the patient's release.

Does a mentally ill patient have any special rights when involuntarily committed for psychiatric treatment?

Yes. The U.S. Supreme Court has upheld the legal right of mentally ill patients hospitalized in a public institution to receive adequate patient care and psychiatric treatment.

To qualify as adequate treatment, the institution must provide or require the following:

- An adequate staff, both in number and qualification
- A facility that offers an adequate diet, comfortable housing, and reasonable recreation
- Patient's informed consent before any unusual treatment
- Payment for work performed for the patient
- An individual treatment plan designed for the patient

The overall standard is that the institution must provide a program designed for rehabilitation rather than incarceration.

What specific protection does the mentally ill patient have relative to sexual rights?

There have been several important cases regarding the rights of mentally ill patients on sexual issues.

The courts, for example, have consistently held that mentally ill individuals have full rights to marry, have children, use contraception, grant consent to abortion and sterilization, and otherwise enjoy the same rights to privacy as afforded competent individuals.

Does a patient being examined by a doctor of the opposite sex have the right to have another person of the patient's sex present in the examining room during an examination?

Yes. Most specialists in obstetrics and gynecology are men. Most routinely have a female nurse with them during all physical examinations. The reason generally given is to protect themselves from a possible charge by the woman patient of improper advances. If the doctor's practice is not to have another female present, however, a woman does have the right to request that another female be present during the examination if she so desires. If the doctor refuses this request in a hospital setting, his method of practice is open to serious ethical question, and his conduct should be immediately reported to the chief of his service.

Is a prisoner entitled to the same quality of health care as other patients?

Even a convicted prisoner does not forfeit all constitutional rights. Among those retained are the Fourteenth Amendment right that guarantees equal protection under the Constitution and the Eighth Amendment right that protects against cruel and unusual punishment.

These constitutional safeguards strongly imply that a prisoner is entitled to reasonable medical care during confinement.

Must a hospital admit a nonemergency patient?

No. The general rule is that a nonemergency patient has no absolute right to be admitted to a hospital. This is another way of saying that there is no universal, legally enforceable right to hospital care in the United States.

Some patients have successfully argued that a municipal hospital has an obligation to accept taxpayers from the community. Such rulings remain too rare to constitute established law, however.

Hospitals may refuse patients for a number of reasons. Some hospitals refuse Medicaid patients and patients who, in the view of the hospital, would cause the hospital to lose money. A more common reason for refusal is that the hospital may be at capacity or otherwise incapable of providing the type or scope of patient care required.

Must a hospital render service to everyone who seeks emergency room treatment?

The general rule is that if a true medical emergency is found to exist, a hospital with emergency facilities is required to render service. No completely satisfactory definition of an emergency has been formulated. In general, an emergency is an injury or acute medical condition that is likely to cause death, disability, or serious or permanent illness.

Once emergency care is provided to the point that the patient is stabilized, the hospital may transfer the patient to a more appropriate facility that is better able to provide long-term care.

Does an imprisoned patient have the same rights to medical treatment as a nonimprisoned patient?

Yes. The Eighth Amendment to the U.S. Constitution guarantees all citizens civilized standards and decency against which penal provisions are to be measured.

Among the more common violations in this area are the following:

- Allowing severe deficiencies to exist in staffing, facilities, equipment, or procedures so that inmates are effectively denied adequate medical care

- Repeated or deliberate acts of negligence or neglect
- Preventing inmates from receiving needed treatment
- Failure to allow access to medical specialists needed for a particular treatment

After an emergency care patient begins receiving treatment, may a hospital discontinue treatment?

No. The hospital must continue to provide service until a patient can be transferred to another facility or discharged without harm.

In several cases, a hospital has incurred liability because it prematurely discharged or transferred an emergency care patient. For a hospital to avoid liability, its medical representative must carefully and objectively assess the patient's condition to determine the patient's capability to be transferred. The hospital must then arrange for the appropriate means of transfer, including the attendance of nurses or other health-care personnel if required.

What steps must a hospital take before a patient is considered to be admitted to the hospital?

The question is important because although a hospital may not be duty bound to care for a nonemergency patient, once the hospital has initiated treatment, it has a duty to continue to provide care until the patient can be discharged safely.

The old rule was that the hospital's duty did not arise until the patient was formally admitted, which involved the actual completion of admission forms, because an initial evaluation of the patient's condition was not sufficient action to constitute admission. Recently, however, courts have begun to expand the concept of admission to include many acts by hospital employees, and have warned that "hospitals should be aware that virtually any act on behalf of the patient will constitute admission and assumption of the duty to treat."

Two cases in which no admission forms were signed illustrate this point. In one case, dressing the patient in a hospital gown in order to make an examination was found sufficient to constitute admission. In another, the actions of a nurse in attempting to contact a doctor to care for the patient was sufficient to constitute assumption on the part of the hospital of the responsibility for the patient's health.

If you are a nurse practicing in an emergency room, you should follow clearly defined hospital protocol in managing initial contacts with patients. If such protocol does not exist, you may request that a policy be designed.

Does a hospital physician or nurse have an obligation to treat a patient with an emergency condition even if hospital policy requires a down payment or prepayment before treatment, and the patient is unable to pay?

Yes. Several states have addressed the issue of cost in statutes obligating hospitals to extend emergency aid. In one state, the law requires that the hospital must "not before admission question the patient or any member of his or her family concerning insurance, credit or payment of charges, provided however, that the patient or a member of his or her family shall agree to supply such information promptly after the patient's admission."

Even when a state statute does not specifically mandate treatment, the trend in case law is to impose an obligation on hospitals to provide emergency care without discussion of financial considerations.

Can a hospital refuse emergency care to a patient who has failed to pay a past hospital bill?

No. An uninsured patient with a poor credit history cannot be denied emergency treatment. If he is refused treatment, the hospital will be liable if the patient's condition becomes significantly worse as a result of the refused care.

Can a hospital legally restrain a competent patient who decides to leave the hospital AMA (against medical advice)?

No. Any attempt to detain or restrain a competent patient would constitute false imprisonment and therefore be actionable.

Generally, the courts disapprove of detaining a patient arbitrarily or for an unreasonably long term or through use of force. Some of these cases occurred when hospitals refused departure to patients until a hospital bill was paid. A hospital can, however, reasonably delay a patient's discharge until routine paperwork is completed. This paperwork would include the patient's signing a form stating that he is leaving against medical advice.

Should a hospital's policy manual indicate how to handle patients who leave the hospital against medical advice?

Absolutely. The policy manual should say under what conditions a patient may be detained, for how long, by what restraints, and by whom. The policy, of course, must conform to applicable state laws and court rulings.

Are there situations where a hospital can lawfully physically restrain a patient from leaving the hospital against medical advice?

Three types of patient can be physically restrained from leaving a hospital:

1. The patient with a communicable disease: leprosy, smallpox, typhoid, and certain sexually transmitted diseases defined by state statute
2. The violent patient who has clearly shown signs that he would be a threat to himself or others if released
3. The psychiatric or mentally incompetent patient who cannot rationally make the decision to leave or care for himself adequately should he leave

What should I do if a patient leaves the hospital against medical advice and refuses to sign an AMA (against medical advice) form?

Although this situation should be covered by the hospital policy manual, if you are faced with this problem, you should be certain that the patient is told that he is leaving against medical advice and the risks involved in so doing, and that he understands that he can return to the hospital. Preferably, this recital should be made in the presence of witnesses.

Generally, you will be required to file an incident report and notify the nursing supervisor and the patient's physician of the patient's decision.

Does a hospital have an obligation to provide routine discharge care to a patient leaving the hospital AMA (against medical advice)?

Yes. Even if a patient is leaving AMA, his rights to discharge planning and discharge care are the same as for other patients. Therefore, the patient should be provided wheelchair service (if required), escort to the hospital's front door, and other medical or nursing follow-up care.

Several cases suggest that a hospital's duty extends to arranging transportation for the patient, particularly if there is a question whether the patient is capable of arranging for his own transportation.

Under what circumstances can a patient be forced to leave the hospital against his will?

This has been called the problem of *premature discharge*. The general rule is that no patient may be discharged except by written order of a doctor who is familiar with the patient's condition. If the patient disagrees with the order, he has a right to demand a consultation with another physician before the order is carried out. In any event, the decision to discharge must be made on the basis of the patient's medical condition and may not take into consideration the patient's nonpayment of past medical bills or consideration of diagnoses related groups (DRG) payments.

In recent years, DRG reimbursement has encouraged

hospitals to discharge patients prematurely, and this will undoubtedly cause an increase in malpractice actions citing premature discharge.

Does the hospital have an obligation to see to it that a patient arrives home safely?

Possibly. The discharge of a patient who is apparently unable to reach home safely because of age or disability could constitute negligence if such patient met with an injury on leaving the hospital. The appropriate standard of care may require that the hospital provide transportation or arrange for a suitable escort for such a patient.

Nursing diagnosis, based on appropriate assessment and carefully documented, is essential immediately before the discharge of a patient.

As a nurse, am I responsible for ensuring a patient's rights to information concerning his medical care?

You do have an evolving role in protecting a patient's rights, but there is little case law that defines the nurse's specific role in upholding a patient's rights to information. Arguably, the primary responsibility falls on the physician and the hospital, rather than on the nurse or other allied health professionals, who are viewed as providing a supportive role.

3

Malpractice Principles

It is impossible to fully understand the application of malpractice principles without first having a firm understanding about the law of negligence. In practice, most malpractice cases involve negligence. There can be other bases for a lawsuit, such as assault and battery or invasion of privacy, which involve claims of a different nature, but these are statistical rarities in nursing practice.

Because of the large percentage of cases based on negligence, lawyers and most laypeople tend to use the words *negligence* and *malpractice* interchangeably. Although every act of professional negligence may be malpractice, it does not necessarily follow that every act of malpractice is negligence.

In this chapter we explore the more common questions on the broader principles of malpractice and liability. With this background, you will be well prepared to apply these principles to everyday practice situations.

Are the number of malpractice cases against nurses increasing?

There has been a dramatic increase. In 1976, fewer than 1000 nurse-related malpractice cases were filed. By 1978, the annual rate had increased to nearly 4000 cases. By 1987, the number of cases (an estimated figure) reached more than 10,000. And the number of cases is expected to continue to grow in the years ahead.

Why has there been a rapid increase in malpractice litigation against nurses?

The growth in malpractice cases against nurses parallels this same litigation explosion against physicians and other professionals. Certainly one reason is the general climate of litigation and the increased resort to lawsuits to resolve real or perceived grievances.

The professional growth of nursing offers a second reason for increased litigation. As nursing continues to grow in terms of responsibility and complexity, it must reciprocally carry with it increased professional accountability.

A third reason is that with increasing complexity of care and the increasing specialization necessary to carry out the care, patients are attended to by many professionals. Fragmentation of care leads to a depersonalization of care, and patients are more apt to sue when they have only transitory relationships with their health-care providers.

Within what category of law is malpractice found?

Malpractice derives from the general category of civil law called the *law of torts*. A "tort" is a legal wrong committed by one person against the person or property of another. To compensate for such a private legal wrong, the law permits the harmed person to bring a civil action against the wrongdoer to recover a sum of money equivalent to the damages incurred.

A tort may be an intentional wrong, such as assault,

battery, false imprisonment, libel, or invasion of privacy, or an unintentional wrong, such as negligence. The one thing all torts have in common is that the person or persons who have been wronged have the legal right to institute a civil action (i.e., a lawsuit) against the person (or legal combination of persons) who caused the wrong. Torts do not include claims arising from breach of contract, however; this is another broad body of law within the general category of civil law.

There are many kinds of torts, but the one that relates most directly to the basic subject of this course is the tort of negligence. Negligence law is a broad field of law that includes many types of negligent conduct in carrying out one's legal responsibilities to others. It embraces the area commonly referred to as malpractice law, which encompasses the negligent conduct of physicians, dentists, nurses, pharmacists, lawyers, and other professionally trained persons.

What is meant by common law, or case law? How does it differ from statutory law?

Legislative bodies cannot possibly enact statutes to cover all forms of human conduct, and thus gaps in the law must be filled by court decision or "common" law, or case law, as it is often called. The second source of law that regulates human social conduct is expressed in judicial decisions that interpret legal issues raised in disputes before the court. This judge-made law is referred to as common law to distinguish it from the more formal type of law expressed in statutes and legislative enactments. Although common law and statutory law are derived from different sources, they are of equal importance and legal effect.

Negligence, for example, which is the basis for most

malpractice cases, has been defined primarily by case law, or common law, although certain provisions, such as reimbursable damages or the statute of limitations for commencing suit, may be governed by statutory law.

How does *negligence* differ from *malpractice*?

Malpractice is used to refer to the negligent acts of persons engaged in professions or occupations in which highly technical or professional skills are employed. *Negligence* is the general term embracing all negligent acts; *malpractice* is the specific term used in referring to negligent conduct in the rendering of professional services by a person with professional education and training. In this sense, malpractice is professional negligence.

The term malpractice may also include wrongful acts other than negligence, such as assault and battery, invasion of privacy, or libel.

What is the general definition of negligence?

At law, every person, whether layman or professional and whether engaged in the simplest or most complex activity is always responsible for conducting himself or herself in a reasonable and prudent manner. A person who fails to act in this required manner and thereby does harm to another is legally "negligent."

A person whose negligence causes harm or injury to the person or property of another may be legally required to pay a sum of money to that person.

The word "negligence," as used in malpractice law, is not necessarily the same as "carelessness." Conduct that is careless is usually negligent, but one can be held negligent in the legal sense even when acting carefully. Here is a simple illustration: If you as a nurse attempt a nursing procedure for which you have no prior training, and you do it as carefully as you know how, your conduct may nevertheless be deemed negligent if harm results to your patient because you did not adhere to the requisite standard of care. The fact that you were careful in carrying out the procedure is considered immaterial from the legal standpoint.

What are the basic elements to be proven in a malpractice suit alleging negligence?

Every nursing malpractice suit includes the following basic elements: (1) a claim that the nurse owed the patient a special duty of care; (2) a claim that the nurse was required to meet a specific standard of care in carrying out the nursing act or function in question; (3) a claim that the nurse failed to meet the required standard of care; and (4) a claim that harm or injury resulted, for which compensation is sought.

For the patient to prevail in a malpractice claim, each of these elements must be proved.

How does a court or jury determine whether the nurse acted in a reasonable manner and was therefore not negligent?

In a nursing malpractice case, the key question whether the nurse acted with reasonable care is ordinarily a matter that requires the opinions of expert witnesses. This is so because members of the jury are laymen and cannot be expected to know of their own accord what nursing skills or procedures should have been followed in the case at hand. Accordingly, the plaintiff must introduce the testimony of one or more experts to prove the applicable standard of care and thereby help the jury decide what a reasonable nurse would have done in the given situation.

Either party may also introduce into evidence medical or nursing texts, the state's nurse practice act, accreditation standards, and other professional references to suggest the prevailing standard of care.

The jury is not ordinarily permitted to decide the issue of a nurse's alleged negligence without some expert testimony concerning the applicable standard of care. If no expert testimony on this issue is introduced by the plaintiff, the court must direct a verdict in favor of the defendant nurse.

How much evidence must a plaintiff have in a malpractice case to sustain the burden of proof that malpractice occurred?

In order to sustain the burden of proof in a malpractice case, the plaintiff must prove his case by a "preponderance of the evidence." This means that he must introduce enough credible (believable) evidence to persuade the jury (or court) that all the essential allegations of his complaint are more probably true than not. If the evidence is evenly balanced on both sides or if it favors the defendant more than the plaintiff, the latter has not sustained the burden of proof and will lose the case.

What factors may a court consider in determining the "reasonableness" of a nurse's action and whether it violated the standard of care?

The surrounding circumstances that are normally considered are (1) the nature and complexity of the nursing function involved; (2) the nurse's known or presumed professional qualifications to perform that function; and (3) the urgency of the overall situation. All these factors play a vital part in every malpractice suit and may be taken into account in determining what is and what is not negligent conduct.

How do the courts define the standard of care I or any other nurse owes a patient?

The courts have generally expressed the nurse's legal duty of care in the following manner: In her performance of her professional duties, a nurse is required to exercise the degree of care and skill that a reasonably prudent nurse with similar training and experience would exercise under the same or similar circumstances.

If you fail to exercise the required degree of care and skill, this failure will be considered negligence, and you will be held legally liable to the person harmed by your negligent conduct.

Will a new inexperienced nurse be held to the same standard of care as older or more experienced nurses?

The fact that a nurse is inexperienced will not, in and of itself, exempt her from liability for negligence in carrying out her nursing duties. This fact emphasizes the need for nursing students to become fully aware of their legal responsibilities in caring for patients, since their age and relative inexperience as nurses will not shield them from liability in a malpractice suit.

As a result, would my failure to comply with standard hospital procedure or a physician's standing order necessarily be a violation of the standard of care owed to my patients?

Not necessarily. Your failure to comply with a standard hospital procedure or a physician's standing order would certainly appear to be evidence of failure to exercise reasonable care, but this is not necessarily the case. Under some circumstances, your rigid adherence to a particular standard procedure or a physician's standing order might actually be considered unreasonable or even dangerous.

You are supposed to be aware of the total nursing needs of your patient, and if you carry out an order that you know is wrong and is likely to be harmful to the patient, you will be held legally liable for so doing. In the eyes of the law, you as a nurse must consider your patient's welfare to be paramount over any standard procedure or method of conduct.

The key to making a decision to deviate from protocol is having knowledge of current quality practice and of appropriate ways to obtain change in protocol or in physicians' orders.

It must also be remembered that certain states do not allow "standing orders" that have not been individualized for the patient.

Is the professional standard of care the same for all kinds of nurses?

No. As a rule, each type of nurse must comply with the standard of care recognized for the professional level or specialization within which she practices. Therefore, RNs are held to the standard of care of a reasonably prudent and competent RN. For example, RNs who have specialized in an area of practice or who have continued their education to a master's or doctor's degree are held to a higher standard of care than RNs without such additional training.

Because you may have specialized training and narrow experience within one area, it is possible that you may no longer feel qualified to practice in other areas. Under these circumstances, you would have both the right and obligation to refuse service in practice areas in which you no longer feel competent.

This point is well recognized by the various specialty groups within the ANA, who have established specific standards of care for their respective specialties.

Will a nursing student be held to a lower standard of care than the standard of care expected from an RN?

When a nursing student has performed duties that are customarily performed only by an RN, the courts have held the nursing student to the higher standard of care of the registered nurse. This rule applies even though the duties may have been specifically assigned to the nursing student by her supervisor. The reason is that patients have the right to assume that all professional services furnished in the hospital, including care provided by nursing students, will be provided by persons with the requisite degree of skill and competence.

As is true of all nurses, nursing students can—and

should—refuse to carry out a specific procedure unless convinced they can do so properly.

What is the role of the ANA in setting professional standards for nurses?

Until 1971, individual hospitals determined nursing practice standards according to prevailing local standards. In 1973, however, the ANA published its own nursing standards, which have since won national acceptance superseding local standards. The ANA Standards of Nursing Practice have since been developed for nurses practicing in specialty areas such as medical–surgical nursing, critical-care nursing, and community health nursing.

The ANA has been active in other areas as well. In 1955, the ANA published a guide for nurses and licensing legislation; in 1970 and 1979, the ANA broadened the scope of nursing practice by expanding the rights of nurses to diagnose.

What is meant by *specialty standards*?

Since 1974, each of the ANA's divisions of nursing practice (geriatrics, community health, maternal–child, mental health, and medical–surgical) has established distinct standards for its specialized practice area. The ANA Congress refers to these as *specialty standards*.

These specialty standards may be adopted by courts when imposing a requisite standard of care on nurses practicing in these areas.

What happens when local and national practice standards differ? Which do the courts give precedence to?

The courts must then determine which standard will apply to the case. Most states now use national standards rather than local standards; this may be required by statutory law or by increasingly common court precedent. A few states still rely on local standards, however. Most hospitals and nurses should seek to have their standards parallel the broader national standards.

Can a departure from established hospital policy be evidence of negligence?

Yes. The generally accepted rule is that staff actions that depart from established institutional policies and procedures constitute a breach of duty. Therefore, it is important for nurses both to be aware of hospital policy and to follow it.

It must be noted, however, that hospital policy does not constitute law, and there may be extenuating cases where hospital policy must be bypassed. Under these circumstances, a nurse must balance her duty to the patient with her duty to the hospital.

If I am fatigued after long, strenuous nursing hours, will the court take this into consideration in a malpractice claim?

Under ordinary circumstances, your claim that you were fatigued and unable to act with your customary degree of care and judgment would not be a relevant factor in your defense in a malpractice suit.

Circumstances relating to your personal state of mind or physical condition are generally considered irrelevant when your liability in a given situation is being determined. Since you are charged with responsibility for your patient's welfare, you are expected to maintain yourself in a physical and mental condition that will enable you to meet your normal professional responsibilities at all times.

How important is continuing education in maintaining my professional competency?

Several studies disclose a high correlation between continuing education and a low incidence of malpractice claims.

Ignorance of new procedures is no excuse for substandard nursing care. And with newer technologies being introduced at a record pace, it is quite easy for all but the most diligent nurse to be left behind.

Attending clinical programs and inservice seminars, and reading professional journals, are important aids in avoiding liability.

Can non-nursing witnesses be used as "experts" to establish a due standard of care in a nursing malpractice case?

Courts often allow physicians, administrators, and other non-nurses to testify when they are qualified by education or experience to recite how nurses typically perform in a stated circumstance.

What qualifies a witness as an "expert" in a malpractice case?

To qualify as an expert witness, the court must be convinced that the witness has the requisite education, experience, or background to speak authoritatively on what he or she is expected to testify about. Often, an expert witness is defined as someone with a superior knowledge on a subject.

Quite often, an expert witness has qualified as an "expert" in other court cases, and this is generally accepted by subsequent courts as sufficient proof of expertise.

What is meant by the doctrine of *res ipso loquitor*?

Res ipso loquitor, translated literally, means "the thing speaks for itself." It is a legal theory of recovery applied in a negligence suit in which the plaintiff cannot prove the defendant's negligence, but the resulting injury could have happened only as a result of the defendant's negligence. For example, if a surgical sponge is found in a patient, common sense would hold that the sponge was not left behind in the patient unless someone was negligent.

Let's assume that I accidentally gave a patient the wrong drug, but the patient suffered no injury. Would I still be liable?

No. The plaintiff must prove by a preponderance of the evidence that he suffered some compensable harm or injury as a result of the defendant's conduct. Negligent conduct or an accident that does not cause any harm or injury reducible to monetary terms will not give rise to legal liability.

Our concept of civil law is to compensate the plaintiff for injuries sustained, not to punish the defendant for unintentional error.

Is the mere fact that a patient suffers further injury (e.g., a post-partum infection) sufficient to prove malpractice?

No. Not every unfavorable medical event is preventable, nor is every such event automatically the basis of a malpractice suit. The law does not expect a nurse to be a guarantor against harm to a patient. The law merely requires that a nurse exercise the degree of care other reasonably prudent nurses would exercise under the circumstances in caring for their patients.

What is meant by *contributory negligence*?

As we noted earlier, the law imposes a duty on every person to act with reasonable care; a person who does not do so is negligent. This legal principle applies to the patient's conduct as well as to the nurse's conduct, and it gives rise to what is known as the *rule of contributory negligence*, which may be stated as follows: When a patient's failure to exercise reasonable care aggravates an injury initially caused by a nurse's negligence, the patient may not be permitted to recover damages. In some states, a patient's contributory negligence will nevertheless permit some recovery, proportionately reduced to the patient's degree of negligence. This is equally true when the patient also contributes to the cause of his injury through his own negligent conduct.

The "reasonableness" of a patient's conduct will be measured against what a prudent individual (layman) would have reasonably done under the same circumstances.

Let's assume that I am being sued along with other nurses and physicians. Can the court apportion damages among the various defendants?

Many states now permit damages to be apportioned among multiple defendants, the extent of liability depending on the jury's determination of each defendant's relative contribution to the harm done.

Can a patient recover for alleged mental trauma if a negligent treatment otherwise causes no physical damage or injury?

Mental trauma without physical injury is no cause for suit in most states. The reason for this is that mental trauma cannot readily be verified, thereby allowing false claims. In recent years, however, more states have begun to recognize mental trauma and have increasingly awarded damages. This trend is likely to continue.

Wrongful acts, such as assault, battery, and defamation, may create liability for mental trauma, since the wrongful act was intentionally committed and intentionally induced trauma is compensable.

Does a fetus inherit a right to sue for injury caused to it during the pregnancy?

The prevailing law is that a person can sue for injuries sustained during the fetal stage provided the fetus was viable at the time of injury (usually within the second trimester) and is subsequently born with injuries.

When does a statute of limitations begin to run?

In many states, the statute of limitations begins to run when the negligent act occurs and regardless of when the patient discovered the negligent act.

The prevailing trend, however, is for states to say that the statute of limitations begins to run when the patient discovered (or should reasonably have discovered) the negligent act, notwithstanding that this may be many years after the negligent act occurred. On that basis, a nurse can never be certain that the statute of limitations has expired, particularly when a negligent act is not immediately apparent.

For a minor, the statute of limitations does not begin to run until he or she reaches the majority age (usually 18 years). This is based on the fact that a minor does not have standing to bring an action in his own name while a minor. Of course, a parent or legal guardian has the right to sue on behalf of a minor, but if the parent does not sue, the minor can do so on reaching adulthood.

Can a court extend the statute of limitations?

Generally, a court is powerless to extend the statute of limitations when the time for filing has clearly expired.

One exception, however, is when a nurse (or other professional) used fraud or falsehood to conceal from the patient information that would lead to the discovery of malpractice. In most concealment cases, the law says that the concealment must be an overt act and not simply the omission of an act. While a nurse cannot actively hide evidence of malpractice, it appears that a nurse has no corresponding duty to expose it. Should a nurse conceal evidence of malpractice, however, a court may extend the time for filing suit to equal the period of concealment.

Is a mentally incompetent person subject to the same rules as a minor relative to the statute of limitations?

Most states give special consideration to mentally incompetent patients. Generally, the statute of limitations does not begin to run until the patient recovers from his mental incompetence, although some states strictly apply the statute of limitations when the patient has a legal guardian or conservator who could have acted in a timely manner on the patient's behalf.

Is it possible that a patient may have a shorter statute of limitations within which to sue a physician than he would have to sue a nurse?

Possibly. Some states impose a shorter statute of limitations on physicians (under a state's medical malpractice law) than they impose on nurses, who typically fall under the longer personal-injury statute of limitations.

Under what circumstances can I as a nurse be held criminally liable for negligently causing the death of a patient?

For negligently caused death to be criminal, the acts would have to be "wanton, wilfull and reckless" conduct.

This means that you performed treatment totally disregarding the welfare and safety of your patient. This does not mean actual intent, but rather an extreme case of negligent conduct. Only at this point can a case for manslaughter exist. Any lesser degree of negligence is only civil in nature.

What should I do if I am sued?

If you are covered by your employer's insurance company, you should immediately contact the legal services administrator at work. This person will then instruct you about how to proceed.

If you have your own insurance coverage, you should carefully review your policy to determine who to contact. Generally, a nurse who is being sued should send a copy of the lawsuit to both the insurance underwriter and the insurance agent who placed the coverage. You should mail the lawsuit by certified mail to ensure receipt, and you should expect to be contacted by the insurance underwriter or their attorneys in advance of the date a defense is due to be filed in court.

As a nurse, should I ever contact the patient who is suing me?

No. You should not try to placate the patient because such attempts are usually unsuccessful. Moreover, any statement made by you can later be used in court.

In fact, you should never discuss the case with anyone but your attorney. This will help avoid information leaks that may compromise the case. And you should never mention the case to colleagues or co-workers so as to protect your professional reputation.

Are some patients more likely than others to bring a malpractice suit?

There is one type of patient who is more likely than any other to bring suit for malpractice when something goes wrong in the treatment process. He is often referred to as the "suit-prone" patient. Because this person's psychological makeup breeds resentment and dissatisfaction in all phases of his life, he poses a serious malpractice threat to all health personnel who have occasion to treat him. Nurses should learn to recognize the symptoms of the suit-prone patient and make appropriate allowance for his emotional needs.

The concept of suit-prone means that this type of person frequently chooses to express his dissatisfaction or resentment by filing a lawsuit against the person who is the object of his dissatisfaction.

The attitudes of the suit-prone patient reflect a basic immaturity that is revealed in all aspects of his life. He is an insecure person and expresses his insecurity by being hostile and uncooperative. Perhaps the thing that characterizes him best is his need to shift blame to other persons as a way of coping with his own inadequacies.

What are some characteristics of a suit-prone patient?

The suit-prone patient, by his very nature, is likely to be an uncooperative patient. He frequently fails to state his complaints accurately and will not follow a prescribed therapeutic regimen. He reacts to his feelings of inferiority and insecurity by being difficult and negative in his dealings with medical personnel.

The suit-prone patient is less likely to sue for malpractice unless he has been badly treated—in the emotional sense—before the act of malpractice. Recognizing the suit-prone patient, therefore, and making proper allowance for his emotional needs in an intelligent manner can effectively eliminate one of the principal causes of malpractice suits. Dealing with persons who have unusual emotional needs calls for patience and genuine understanding on the part of the nurse. It is a challenge to which every nurse should rise, knowing that success will make her chosen career a much more satisfying one from every point of view.

As a nurse, should I ever admit an error to a patient?

No. If you believe you have committed an error, you should discuss it only with your nursing supervisor, hospital administrator, or legal counsel for the hospital.

Obviously, admitting an error to a patient or a patient's family may cause unnecessary concern and, of course, increase the likelihood of a lawsuit. Moreover, an admission of an error or of negligence can be used as evidence in a subsequent malpractice case.

How should I handle a suit-prone patient?

Special attention must be paid to the patient who is suit-prone. In fact, it is one of the few things you can do to prevent a later malpractice suit by such a person. Paying special attention to the suit-prone patient means being aware of the way he reacts to illness, his attitude toward doctors and nurses, and his hidden fears and antagonisms. It means helping him to deal with his depression or fear, showing interest and sympathy to his pain and suffering, and expressing appreciation for his efforts to cooperate in the recommended course of treatment.

You are making a mistake if you are insensitive to the suit-prone patient's unusual psychological needs. Indifference to the patient only adds fuel to his preexisting feelings of resentment, setting the stage for a later lawsuit.

How can a "patient-centered" approach to nursing care reduce my liability?

The current emphasis on patient-centered treatment is based on the philosophy that as a nurse, you should interact with the patient as a human being instead of simply doing things for him (or to him) in a stereotyped manner. The patient, in turn, should be encouraged to understand and participate in his care, thereby assuming a degree of responsibility for the outcome of that care.

With the focus on the patient rather than the task, the interaction between nurse and patient becomes more personal, less businesslike, and more satisfying to both patient and nurse. Obviously, patients are less likely to sue a nurse with whom a good relationship has been established.

What should I do when a patient asks my opinion of his condition?

You should never offer an opinion about a patient's condition or prognosis. Such a practice can be construed as making a diagnosis and therefore practicing medicine without a license. Moreover, the patient may hold you responsible when the medical outcome is different from that which you portrayed.

Why are some very excellent nurses, with high professional skills, often sued for malpractice, while less proficient nurses experience fewer problems?

Some nurses have great technical competence, but they find it difficult to establish warm or friendly relationships with others. They may show their uneasiness with close person-to-person contacts by being authoritarian, aloof, or so busy with the mechanics of nursing care that they have little time for meaningful human interaction. It should be recognized that such personality patterns on the part of nurses may be important causes of later malpractice suits.

Understanding patients' attitudes and behaviors will not only prevent malpractice suits but will stimulate a patient's participation in his treatment, thus making the treatment more effective.

Are there any broad guidelines for me to follow if I am to avoid liability?

There are five baseline standards to observe:

1. Practice within the scope of the nurse practice act.
2. Observe the hospital's and department's policy manuals.

3. Measure up to established practice standards.
4. Always put the patient's rights and welfare first.
5. Develop and maintain a good interpersonal relationship with each patient and his or her family.

Doesn't my employer's insurance coverage provide adequate protection to me as a nurse?

The practical problem of relying on your employer's coverage is that the insurance company may not be obligated to defend or pay a judgment on behalf of the employee. Other questions also arise:

- How will you pay the costs of defending yourself if the hospital's insurer refuses to defend you?
- What protection do you have if your employer's insurer takes the position that your employer is not liable for your acts as occurring beyond the scope of your employment?
- How can you be protected by your employer's insurance if the insurance was canceled?
- What if your employer does not carry enough insurance, leaving you unprotected against any claim for a large amount?

Obviously, these potential problems can be avoided only if you carry your own insurance.

What risks do I run by having no insurance coverage?

Since many nurses do not have substantial assets, they may decide to "go bare" and not buy insurance. They may decide that they have few personal assets to lose even if they are sued, so why go to the expense of insurance?

For these nurses, a malpractice suit may be more readily dismissed once the plaintiff realizes the nurse is without insurance; other, more stubborn cases can be dismissed through bankruptcy.

Considering the relatively low cost of nursing insurance, however, it is an extremely good investment even if you have few personal assets to protect.

Does a malpractice policy cover all forms of negligence?

The policy will define the types of errors covered. Ordinarily, the policy will be broad enough to cover all types of negligence arising from nursing practice; however, the coverage may not extend to services not arising from professional employment or services beyond the scope of your employment.

Insurance does not cover all sources of liability. In some cases, the exclusions are stated within the policy. Most often mentioned as uninsured are the following:

- Assault and battery
- Defamation
- Invasion of privacy
- False imprisonment
- Intentional wrongdoing
- Acts that involve a violation of law or regulation

Unfortunately, these exclusions can be important because it is possible that your liability may result from excluded acts.

Are there specific items I should check for in my malpractice policy?

You should specifically check to see if there is the following coverage:

- Coverage when nurses under your care are negligent
- Coverage for failure to instruct patients properly
- Coverage for errors in medication administration
- Coverage for errors in reporting or recording
- Coverage for misuse of equipment
- Coverage for private-duty nursing
- Coverage for volunteer service

What factors determine the cost of a malpractice policy?

The cost of insurance depends on many variables.

The major factor is the amount of coverage. A $500,000 policy will obviously cost more than a $100,000 policy, but not necessarily five times as much because of the reduced probability of the higher award.

A co-deductible can significantly lower premiums; the higher the deductible, the greater the savings will be.

Geography and the type of nursing practice both influence policy costs because each influences the probability of a claim being filed. Nurses in California, for example, are more likely to be sued than are nurses in Maine. Emergency room nurses have a higher incidence of claims than do general-duty nurses.

Nurses who have experienced prior claims may also face higher premiums.

Nurses may find that they can greatly reduce premiums by buying insurance on a "group" rate, through nursing associations, or by simply comparing the rates of several companies.

What is the difference between a "single limits" and a "double limits" insurance policy?

In a "single limits" policy, you buy coverage in set dollar increments, for example, $100,000 or $200,000. In the less common "double limits" policy, you buy insurance in a combination package, such as $100,000–$300,000. In a "double limits" policy, the smaller sum is what the insurance company will pay to any one plaintiff; the larger sum is the amount it will pay on any one incident regardless of the number of plaintiffs. Most malpractice insurance policies are "double limits."

What is meant by a "claims made" insurance policy?

Some policies cover claims regardless of when the suit was filed. Others structure their policies to cover claims actually made within the year of coverage, even though the negligent act occurred several years earlier. This is known as a "claims made" policy. It helps the insurance company because it can determine the extent of its potential liability at the close of the insurance year. The company is not responsible for claims filed later, even though the negligent act took place during the year of coverage.

You would generally enjoy no advantage with a "claims made" policy unless you wanted coverage for errors made in previous years when you may not have had insurance coverage. Conversely, with a "claims made" policy, you would be without coverage in later years unless you continued to renew your coverage.

How does a "co-deductible" work in an insurance policy?

If a malpractice policy has a deductible of $2500, then the insurance company is obligated to pay an award in excess of that amount. As the insured, you have to pay the first $2500 under the claim.

Frequently, an insurance company will offer the insured the right to select the amount of the deductible. As the deductible increases, the premium is reduced, since a larger part of the risk is being paid by the insured.

What are the duties of an insurance company when a malpractice claim is filed?

The insurance company has to defend against the claim, even if the claim exceeds the amount of coverage. In addition, the insurer must pay any award up to the amount of the policy, less any deductible.

An insurance company has the obligation to act reasonably and in "good faith" to protect its insured. If an offer of settlement is negligently or in "bad faith" declined, causing excess liability to the insured, the insured has the right to force the insurance company to pay the "excess," even beyond the policy limit.

Should I investigate my insurance coverage before I donate nursing services as a volunteer?

Yes. You should review whether your existing policy offers protection for volunteer activities and whether the coverage is adequate. Further, you should discover what insurance protection is available from the sponsoring organization.

May my insurance company settle a nursing malpractice claim without my consent?

That depends on the terms of your insurance policy. In most insurance contracts, the insurance company reserves the right to compromise or settle any claims or lawsuits.

Many malpractice policies contain a clause that gives the health-care provider the right to reject the insurer's decision to settle the case. An insurance company that then settles a malpractice action (without the consent of the provider who has such a policy) would be guilty of a breach of contract and liable for any damages.

Nevertheless, if you unreasonably refuse to settle a claim, and the insurance company loses the suit, the insurance company's liability is typically limited to the prior settlement offer acceptable to the insurance company. You would be liable for any excess.

What should I do if I am sued for malpractice and I am not covered by insurance?

You must then retain an attorney to prepare your defense. You should probably interview several attorneys experienced in handling medical or nursing malpractice cases. Local and state bar associations usually maintain rosters of attorneys who specialize in this area.

If I am uninsured or underinsured, what steps can I take to protect my property in the event that I lose a malpractice case?

There are many legal ways to protect property in the event of a lawsuit. You should discuss them with an attorney experienced in these matters, preferably in advance of a lawsuit if the property is to be protected adequately.

What obligations do I have in working with my insurance company in the defense of a malpractice case?

Your main duty is to cooperate fully with the insurance company to defend the claim. This requires you to communicate and reveal all relevant information; to go to hearings and to answer all forms of discovery; and to take part in, and testify at, the trial. Should you fail to cooperate or undertake acts detrimental to the defense of your case, the insurance company can decline coverage.

At what point am I obligated to tell the insurance company about a potential malpractice claim?

Generally, you are not obligated to tell your insurance company about a possible claim until you are actually sued or a written claim letter is received. Nevertheless, it is wise to involve the insurance company whenever there is a reason to believe a lawsuit will arise. Often, early intervention by the insurance company will prevent the disclosure of damaging evidence, or a favorable settlement may be made directly with the patient before the start of a lawsuit.

How many malpractice cases actually go to trial?

Fewer than 10%. The vast majority of cases are settled out of court, since both plaintiffs and defendants realize that a trial can be costly and can often produce unpredictable results.

Doesn't settlement of a malpractice case constitute an admission of wrongdoing?

No. The law regards settlement only as a compromise between two parties to end a lawsuit and avoid further expense associated with litigation. Similarly, an offer to compromise or settle a claim cannot be considered evidence of liability or an admission of liability.

Can I sue the patient and his attorney for bringing a frivolous malpractice suit against me?

Yes. There are a number of theories on which suit can be brought, and as recently as 1976, they have been hailed by the American Medical Association as a new weapon that could "discourage the filing of frivolous or non-meritorious cases. . . ." Suit can be brought on one or more of four grounds: (1) defamation; (2) malicious prosecution; (3) abuse of process; and (4) legal malpractice.

Recovery on such a countersuit is rare because the nurse must show "bad faith" on the part of the plaintiff (patient), his attorney, or both. "Bad faith" means that the patient knew or should have known he had no realistic likelihood of recovery, but brought the suit primarily to harass or injure the reputation of the nurse.

4

Basic Liability Issues

One authority on nursing care estimates that nurses may be called on to provide more than 7000 nursing procedures. Even if that estimate can be challenged, all nurses recognize that their work presents plenty of opportunities for liability.

It may be impossible to highlight every possibility of liability, and such an effort would be of no practical importance. Statistics prove that the vast majority of malpractice cases arise from relatively few situations. This chapter focuses on several separate but equally important reasons for liability and what steps you can take to avoid it.

At what point should I consider the nurse–patient relationship to have begun?

The nurse–patient relationship is a legal status created the moment you begin to provide nursing care to another person. This relationship is important because of the legal duties and responsibilities attached. Once a nurse–patient relationship is established, you legally owe a special duty of care to your patient that is greater than the general duty of care owed to other persons generally. The failure to meet this special duty of care owed to a patient forms the heart of every malpractice suit against a nurse.

What must you and the patient do or say to create the nurse–patient relationship? No special words, agreements, or contracts are required. The only thing required is the actual provision of nursing services. The fact that the recipient of such services (your patient) may not have requested them, or may even resent them, has no bearing on the legal effect or consequences of your actions. In any case, a nurse–patient relationship will come into being as soon as you undertake what would reasonably be construed as nursing care.

Of course, the nurse–patient relationship also begins when you expressly or impliedly agree or contract to provide nursing care, even though no service has yet been provided.

Are there circumstances when I can legally diagnose?

Some states include diagnosis as part of nursing responsibilities. Several court cases have also taken the position that a nurse may diagnose, particularly when medical intervention cannot be obtained in time. Nevertheless, the interpretation of what diagnosis you can legally conduct remains questionable.

Hospitals and physicians increasingly delegate more authority to nurses, for example, in critical care units (CCUs) and intensive care units (ICUs) where nursing duties inevitably include diagnosis.

Cost containment, the increased use of nurse practitioners, and expanding professional stature for nurses all suggest that nurses will increasingly have the right to diagnose in many more situations. At the present time, however, nurses diagnose "human responses to actual and potential health problems." This is different from the medical prerogative of diagnosing disease.

What should I do if I see another health-team member incorrectly performing a clinical procedure?

You have a duty to stop the procedure and immediately report the incident to your nursing supervisor or immediate superior. This, of course, must be done in as tactful a manner as possible.

Under no circumstances should you continue your involvement in the procedure—even if ordered to do so by a physician.

Must I always carry out a physician's order?

You are legally authorized and required to carry out any nursing or medical procedure that you are directed to carry out by a duly licensed physician, unless you have reason to believe harm will result to the patient from doing so. When there is no reason to question a physician's order, your failure to carry out such an order will subject you to liability for any consequent harm to the patient.

To meet your legal responsibility in carrying out a physician's order, you must know how to execute the procedure in question, as well as what the effect of the procedure should be on the patient.

When you have reason to question a physician's order, you should do so tactfully but directly, keeping in mind the fundamental rule that the patient's safety is always a paramount responsibility.

If you have reason to believe that some harm will come

to the patient if you carry out a physician's order, you have a legal duty not to follow the order. You should bring the matter immediately to the attention of your supervisor (or your instructor, if you are a nursing student). If your supervisor or instructor is not available at the moment, the matter should be brought to the attention of a responsible hospital official.

The safety and security of your patient is your paramount responsibility, although the physician shares this legal responsibility.

Under what circumstances may I perform medical procedures?

Nurses are authorized to perform many acts that, under other circumstances, would constitute the unauthorized practice of medicine. This is particularly true in emergency situations. In addition, you are legally required to carry out any nursing or medical procedure you are directed to carry out by a duly licensed physician, unless you have reason to believe that harm will come to the patient from the execution of the order.

Under no circumstances should you carry out a physician's order that directs you to commit an act that you know, or should know, to be unlawful. If you do commit such an act, you will subject yourself to criminal liability, whether or not the patient suffers injury, and you cannot avoid such liability by claiming that you were merely following the doctor's orders.

It is often difficult to determine what actions would be lawful in specific instances. Nurse licensing boards in most states provide guidance on a case-by-case basis.

Under what circumstances will I be held legally responsible for seeing that no harm comes to my patient?

You are required to exercise ordinary or reasonable care to safeguard and protect your patient from any known or reasonably foreseeable harm. The courts have held this to be as much the nurse's responsibility as that of the physician. Many of your routine patient-care activities as a nurse involve the safety and security of your patient, and you are expected to perform these acts without any special medical order or supervision.

The kind and degree of nursing care necessary to protect a patient from harm will always depend on the particular circumstances of the case. The prime determinant of the type of care necessary to protect the patient adequately is the patient's physical and mental capacity to contribute to his own safety and security.

Who is ultimately responsible for an individual patient's care?

If the referring physician who sent the patient to the hospital is a member of the hospital staff or has staff privileges, he or she will continue to be in charge and is termed the *attending physician*.

If the referring doctor does not have staff privileges, another physician, typically a resident, will be in charge. Problems most commonly arise when patients admitted through a clinic or emergency ward do not know which physician is in charge of their care. Just as the hospital has a specific duty to place a physician in charge of patient care, the patient has a right to know who that physician is.

Do I have a responsibility to bring a patient's deteriorating medical condition to the attention of the medical staff?

Yes. One of your primary responsibilities is the duty to monitor your patient's condition and immediately seek medical intervention should your patent's condition warrant it.

Although several case decisions impose this duty, it is not necessarily clear how it is to be accomplished. In many instances, this reporting consists of verbally notifying the attending physician, or if the physician is unavailable, you can then report the situation to the chief of service.

Merely notifying these authorities is not sufficient, however. You must continue actively to seek intervention until intervention is obtained.

How should I handle ambiguous physician's orders?

Hospital policy and procedure should be followed when you are confronted with vague or ambiguous orders, or with orders that have more than one possible interpretation.

You should always contact the physician as soon as possible and should document his response in clarifying the orders.

You should follow your supervisor's decision on whether to delay treatments pending clarification by the physician.

How should I handle special problems that arise with a mentally ill patient?

Because of their limitations, mentally ill patients often have idiosyncratic needs. A patient, for example, may refuse to shower or insist on smoking where smoking is not permitted.

Whenever a patient insists on making special demands or refuses to cooperate with the routine regimen, the team members who commonly interact with the patient should meet and agree on the approach to be pursued in assisting the patient to live within the constraints imposed by his situation. Team members include the physician, nurses, nursing assistants, the social worker, and therapists from a variety of disciplines. This strategy not only ensures a more balanced approach to the problem but one that is easier to defend.

When can I legally restrain a patient?

A patient can, and should, be restrained whenever the lack of restraint would endanger himself or other patients. In that event, you should employ the degree of restraint necessary to control the procedure while avoiding unduly extreme restraint that may injure the patient. Patients thus restrained frequently need constant supervision to prevent them from incurring injury.

What factors are legally significant in determining the degree of care required to protect a patient from harm?

The nature and quality of nursing care legally required to protect a patient from harm is based not only on the patient's physical condition but on his ability to contribute to his own safety and security. This rule assumes particular importance when the patient is suffering from some form of emotional illness that prevents him from appreciating the risk of harm to which he may be exposed.

When there is neither any previous history nor any present indication that the patient is dangerous to others or to himself, the degree of care and watchfulness expected of the nurse is less. Correspondingly, the degree of alertness must be heightened in cases where suicide has been repeatedly threatened or the patient has known assaultive tendencies or is in a weakened condition related to disease or medication.

Must physical restraint be ordered by the patient's physician?

It is always preferable for a physician to order restraint, but it is not necessary if the need for restraint becomes obvious before physician approval can be obtained.

Of course, the physician should be notified as soon as possible, and he should issue appropriate orders for continued or modified restraint.

May I physically restrain a suicidal patient against the patient's will?

You not only may but often must do so. A suicidal patient is presumed to be without the mental competency to give or withhold consent. Therefore, you must take all reasonable steps to protect the patient from further self-inflicted injury.

You must not, however, use more force than is reasonably necessary to restrain the patient or needlessly abuse or cause the patient harm during the process of restraint.

How should a physician properly document an order for patient restraint?

Many states specifically define the items to be contained in a doctor's restraint order. Typically these include the following:

- The results of the doctor's physical examination of the patient
- A description of the patient's behavior that makes restraint necessary
- The type of restraint to be used
- The period during which the restraint should be used
- An order stating how frequently the patient should be checked

Are there any special nursing requirements for a patient under restraint?

Yes. In caring for a patient under restraint, you must do the following:

1. Assess the patient and monitor and record the patient's vital signs and overall condition together with his level of comfort.
2. Release the patient in restraints every several (usually 2) hours.
3. Feed the patient in restraints in an upright position to minimize his risk in choking on food particles.

You should know applicable state law, and, of course, hospitals should have specific policies on this issue.

What degree of force is permitted to restrain a patient physically?

only the degree of physical force required to achieve restraint. Clearly, excess force that is harmful to the patient can result in a lawsuit against the hospital or nurse involved in the restraint.

When may physical restraints be imposed on patients?

Most states require a physician to write a restraint order and place it in the patient's records before physical restraints can be applied.

In an emergency situation, such as when the patient suddenly and unexpectedly becomes physically abusive, any person may apply reasonable restraints to the patient. In these cases, however, a physician's authorization for continued restraint must be obtained as soon as possible.

You must remember that an order for restraint must be for a specified time period and therefore reviewed at periodic and reasonable intervals. You would also be wise to remain with the patient until the restraint order is obtained, and to observe any restrained patient frequently.

What if I discover a patient is missing from the hospital?

Your first priority is to notify your nursing supervisor immediately. If the patient was in police custody or poses a threat to the public, the police should also be notified immediately. The patient's family should then be notified, and efforts to locate the patient should be maintained until the patient is found. The situation should also be included on the patient's medical chart and documented in an incident report.

Do I have any special responsibility in guarding the postoperative patient?

A recovery room patient should never be left unattended without nursing personnel. The responsibility for the patient remains with the recovery room staff until the patient is turned over to the medical unit staff and appropriate orders have been given.

Whenever possible, an RN should accompany a postoperative patient, particularly a high-risk patient who is being transported from the recovery room to a private room.

What is meant by *understaffing*?

Understaffing is the failure to provide sufficient professionally trained personnel reasonably or adequately to meet the health-care needs of the hospital's patient population.

This has become a central complaint of many nurses and one chronically existing because of the nursing shortage and the financial constraints now affecting most hospitals.

Understaffing can create liability, for it inevitably produces substandard care, increased errors, hasty procedures, poor documentation, and generally questionable patient care.

What constitutes an adequate nurse staffing?

There are no formal guidelines because no state has enacted nurse–patient ratio requirements. The JCAH staffing standard simply says that "nursing personnel staffing shall be sufficient to assure prompt recognition of an untoward change in a patient's condition and to facilitate appropriate intervention by the nursing, medical or hospital staff."

In the absence of clear standards, the courts have decided the issue on a case-by-case basis. Nevertheless, a hospital will be measured against the nurse–patient ratio generally followed by similar hospitals.

As a charge nurse, can I be held liable for understaffing?

You may be found liable for understaffing when, as a charge nurse, you know understaffing exists but fail to notify the hospital administration or take steps within your power to correct it. If the hospital fails to respond to your demands for more personnel, you generally have no further responsibility except to assign your nurses as prudently as possible.

Will a hospital automatically be liable for injuries resulting from understaffing?

No. Hospital liability in this situation is not automatic. If a hospital could have provided adequate staff and failed to do so, it would normally be held liable. If, however, a nurse has suddenly called in sick, thereby requiring another nurse to perform "double duty," the hospital may escape liability under the doctrine of the *sudden emergency exception*, since the hospital had no reasonable way of foreseeing or avoiding the understaffing problem.

How can a hospital avoid liability for understaffing?

Except for the sudden emergency rule, it appears a hospital cannot avoid the possibility of liability from understaffing.

Essentially, a hospital must either hire sufficient nursing personnel to staff an area adequately or else close the area or restrict the patient population to match nursing availability.

What is an acceptable nurse–patient ratio in the recovery room?

The proper ratio depends on the kind of surgical procedure and the patient's resultant condition. Clearly, one nurse would be needed for just one open heart surgery patient, but may this same nurse safely oversee four or five patients with minor surgery?

To answer this question, the nursing ratio should be consistent throughout the day and should be consistent with the ratio at similar hospitals performing comparable surgical procedures.

Will unavailability of nurses be a legitimate defense when hospitals are accused of understaffing?

The courts are reluctant to accept this defense, particularly when the hospital knew it would have staffing problems and continued to admit patients. Courts are also expected to impose a greater duty on a hospital to use temporary nurse agencies to cure staffing problems.

The fact that understaffing was undertaken for economic reasons will not excuse a hospital if its understaffing would likely cause inadequate patient care.

May I refuse to "float"?

Unfortunately, "floating" is necessary in most hospitals. You cannot refuse to float unless you have a union contract that prevents floating, or you can show that you cannot do the work required in a new assignment.

If you are assigned to new duties for which you are unqualified, you should point this out to your supervisor. If your supervisor insists that you perform duties for which you are unqualified, you should refuse. Although refusal can cause dismissal, the few reported dismissals have been overturned once the reasons for refusal have been reported to higher authorities in the hospital.

How should I handle an overload situation?

First, you should make every effort to protest the overload and get the workload reduced. If your supervisor or charge nurse won't provide relief, you may notify the hospital administrator. Finally, you should document your efforts and file a copy of the report with your supervisor or the director of nursing.

You should not, however, walk off the job. Such action may be viewed as patient abandonment, causing other potential liabilities.

Under what circumstances can I be terminated by a hospital?

If you are working without a contract, you can be dismissed for any reason unless

- Your hospital guarantees a right to notice and a hearing before dismissal.
- State laws prevent your employer from retaliating if you report violations to state agencies.
- Your termination was the result of discrimination or a civil rights violation.

What services can I request of a volunteer in the hospital?

Most hospitals define the scope of services that may be performed by a volunteer in their policy manuals.

Nevertheless, even if the required services are within the policy guidelines, you have the responsibility to determine that the volunteer is capable of properly performing the requested services. If there is any doubt about the capability of the volunteer, he should be closely supervised or you should wait for a more experienced volunteer or regular staff member to perform the required task.

At no time should a volunteer be assigned a task that is properly the function of a registered nurse.

Can I be held liable if I use defective equipment that causes a patient harm?

Yes, if you knew, or should have known, about the product defect or had a responsibility to maintain the equipment properly so as to prevent the injury claimed.

Most product-defect cases come under what is called

breach of warranty, which imposes liability only on the hospital, the manufacturer, and others who sold the product in the channel of distribution. Since you are only the agent of the hospital, you would normally have no liability under a "breach of warranty" claim.

How can I avoid liability when I use equipment that can cause burns—for example, electrosurgical equipment, heat pads, and diathermy machines?

You should first determine whether the equipment is working properly. When you use such equipment, you should carry out the procedure carefully and continually observe the patient until the therapy is completed. If the patient is awake, he should be frequently asked whether he is experiencing discomfort.

How can I reduce liability arising from neglect of patient safety?

A patient's physical safety is a primary nursing responsibility.

There are many ways in which a patient's personal safety can be threatened. Nevertheless, risk can be substantially lowered by following these recommendations:

- Report loose, defective, or improperly working equipment immediately, and refrain from using it until it is repaired.
- Water or other substances on the floor should be removed or called to the attention of the housekeeping staff.

- Help weak patients walk, and use proper transfer methods when moving patients.
- Use bedrails and other restraining devices when patient immobilization is required.
- Report any violation of hospital rules (e.g., smoking).

What legal obligation do I have toward patient teaching?

Although most states encourage a nursing role in patient teaching, few states specifically require it.

Generally, reference to patient teaching is found in hospital policies and ethical codes by nursing organizations. The ANA's Standards of Nursing Practice provides, for example, that "the plan of nursing care includes priorities and the prescribed nursing approaches or measures to achieve the goals derived from the nursing diagnoses."

The courts, however, have consistently determined that patients have a right to know about their illness and treatment; therefore, when the right to know becomes critical to the patient's health, a court is likely to view patient teaching as a nursing responsibility and legal duty.

How can patient teaching help reduce nursing liability?

The most direct benefit, of course, is that the patient better understands his treatment and his role in self-care.

Patients taught about their health care are also more cooperative because they recognize the purpose for each treatment and the role it plays in their recovery. They also adapt more readily to changes in treatment.

Last, but certainly not least, patient teaching helps develop a bond of trust and confidence between patient and health-care provider. Through this closer relationship, the patient will be less likely to become hostile; therefore, there will be less likelihood of litigation.

How would a court determine whether I was negligent in my performance of patient teaching?

A court will first consider whether patient teaching was part of your responsibility based on a review of hospital policy manuals or existing custom in the facility.

The court will next determine whether you met the requisite standard. If evidence indicates that you breached your duty to the patient by providing inadequate or wrongful information, or instruction that resulted in harm or injury to the patient, you may be held liable for any resultant injury.

5

Liability in Special Settings

As a nurse, you can easily be exposed to liability while you are off duty or are practicing in a nontraditional setting.

You may well understand what is expected of you when practicing in a hospital; there are ample guidelines, policies, and rules that closely govern your actions. But what about when you're off duty? What are your liabilities as a private-duty nurse or when working as a volunteer? Very few professional guidelines exist to cover these situations adequately, so whether you provide care regularly when off duty or just give advice to your next-door neighbor occasionally, this chapter can answer your questions so that you can stay on a sound legal footing.

Do I have a responsibility to render emergency care to a person outside the hospital, such as in a roadside accident?

Your legal responsibility to provide emergency care to persons within your normal employment setting is quite different from your legal responsibility under other circumstances. In a noncontractual and nontherapeutic setting, you have no legal obligation to render emergency care to someone in need, even though you may have a moral and ethical obligation to render such care. Thus, you cannot be held legally liable for refusing to offer emergency care to the victim of a highway accident or other similar occurrence, no matter how life-threatening the circumstances.

Even though you may be under no legal obligation to provide emergency care to persons who are not within your normal work responsibilities, once you volunteer to give such emergency care, you are legally obligated to do so in a reasonable manner. This simply means that you are expected to act as other, reasonably prudent nurses would act under the same emergency circumstances. Many "Good Samaritan" laws were passed with the hope that the protection afforded nurses would encourage them to render emergency aid.

Do any states compel a health-care provider to come to the rescue of an accident victim?

Vermont, along with many foreign countries, requires any person aware that another is in grave danger to come to his rescue, provided it will not endanger the safety of the rescuer. Minnesota and Wisconsin have similar laws.

When you provide such care, you are held to the standard that would be expected of any nurse in similar circumstances. Obviously, this standard is higher than a standard applied to the actions of a layperson.

Can I be held liable for negligence if I voluntarily perform emergency aid without expecting payment?

Possibly. Payment or providing service for a fee is not needed to maintain a negligence case. A nonpaid volunteer can be equally liable. The "Good Samaritan" law will, however, give greater protection to the nonpaid volunteer because the statutes usually hold practitioners expecting a fee to be exempt from protection under the statutes, provided the treatment otherwise occurred within the scope of the "Good Samaritan" statute.

Is the required standard of care relaxed in an emergency situation, or will I be expected to act with the same skill as in a routine setting?

If you are suddenly and unexpectedly confronted with an emergency situation presenting imminent (perhaps life-threatening) danger to a patient, you are not expected to use the same degree of prudence and judgment that would be required in a calmer, more deliberate setting. In an emergency, your duty is merely to exercise the degree of care and skill that an ordinarily prudent nurse of similar training and experience would exercise under the same emergency circumstances.

Three surrounding circumstances are of primary concern: (1) the nature of the nursing function involved; (2) your qualifications to perform that function; and (3) the urgency of the overall situation.

How real is the danger in administering emergency care at the scene of an accident?

There is apparently little danger. To date, there has not been a single recorded case in which a physician or nurse has been held liable for malpractice involving emergency medical care at the scene of an accident, and the threat of such a suit occurring in the future is considered extremely exaggerated by most legal writers. Therefore, all members of the nursing profession should recognize their ethical and moral obligation to render emergency medical assistance to persons in genuine need of such assistance, without regard to any legal protection offered by state "Good Samaritan" laws. In the final analysis, the giving of reasonable care under the emergency circumstances involved will more than adequately protect you from legal liability for malpractice.

Do any laws protect me if I decide to help an accident victim?

Yes. First, the "Good Samaritan" laws provide protection against negligent acts in most situations. Further, the common-law, or case-law, decisions generally protect a volunteer nurse from ordinary negligence and impose liability only if the nurse was grossly negligent or wanton, wilful, and reckless in her conduct.

Do "Good Samaritan" laws apply if I accept payment for my services?

No. "Good Samaritan" laws do not usually apply in this instance because, by accepting money, you have established a professional relationship with the person aided.

Do "Good Samaritan" laws provide me with the same protection as afforded a physician?

Not necessarily. Some states cover physicians only, not nurses or other health professionals. Further, a state may offer a nurse different protection from that offered a physician.

Will "Good Samaritan" statutes fully protect me if I provide emergency care?

Not necessarily. All but a handful of American states have enacted "Good Samaritan" statutes in order to encourage physicians (and, in some cases, nurses) to render emergency aid to victims of roadside accidents. The typical statute provides that a physician or nurse "shall not be liable for any civil damages as a result of ordinary negligence in rendering such care." In some states, the "Good Samaritan" statute covers only roadside accidents; in others, the statute extends to other "emergencies" as well. Again, in some states, the statute applies to all licensed physicians; in others, it is limited only to physicians licensed in that particular state. Because of the wide differences between states in the scope, applicability, and coverage of these "Good Samaritan" statutes, it is virtually impossible for a physician or nurse to know whether he or she really enjoys legal protection when rendering emergency care in a state that has such a law. Information on this issue is generally available through state nurses' associations. You should be thoroughly familiar with the "Good Samaritan" laws in your state before you volunteer emergency aid.

Will a "Good Samaritan" statute protect me if I provide emergency care in the hospital?

Although the scope of protection depends on the particular state, most "Good Samaritan" laws apply only to aid rendered "outside both the place and course" of professional employment. Many states further limit the protection to "roadside" accidents, implying that only vehicular accidents are covered in those states.

Will "Good Samaritan" laws protect me if I regularly volunteer or donate my services?

No. If you routinely donate your services, such services generally do not qualify for protection under "Good Samaritan" statutes. Further, volunteer services do not typically constitute "emergency services" as defined within these statutes.

Do I have increased authority or responsibility in an emergency situation?

Yes. It is well established that in an emergency situation, you may perform any medical act deemed necessary to preserve life or limb. The reasonableness of your conduct in such a situation is always gauged by the surrounding circumstances, and you are not held to the standard of care expected of you under more normal circumstances. In all cases involving emergency care, you are expected to summon medical assistance as soon as possible, and your legal privilege of making medical judgments and undertaking medical acts in an emergency is limited to those immediately required acts.

When does my responsibility to an accident victim end?

Your responsibility ends in the following circumstances:

- When an authorized emergency medical service (EMS) or rescue service arrives
- When a physician or someone with superior medical qualifications arrives to take over
- When the patient is no longer in need of medical care
- When the patient is pronounced dead

Should you leave an accident victim before one of these events occur, you can be sued for any damage resulting from the abandonment.

What are the most common causes of liability in treating an accident victim?

Although there are no reported cases against nurses who render emergency aid, the most frequent lawsuits against others are based on the following:

- Moving the patient needlessly
- Allowing unskilled personnel to tend or treat the patient
- Leaving the scene before skilled personnel arrive to care for the patient
- Forcing or encouraging the patient to walk

If I render aid in a disaster situation, may I go beyond the traditional limits of authority defined in the state's nurse practice act?

Yes. Nurses commonly are required to perform services in a community disaster that go beyond their traditional duties. You generally can provide substitute or expanded care in disasters based on the same exemption that allows an out-of-state nurse to volunteer her service in a disaster. Moreover, both common sense and regulatory policy will invoke the flexibility needed to allow you to meet the needs of the occasion.

May other health professionals refuse to render emergency care to nonpatients outside the hospital or medical setting?

Ordinarily, yes. It has generally been held that health professionals, like other private citizens, have no legal obligation to come to the aid of their fellow citizens in distress, even life-threatening distress. The real reasons some professionals do not render aid probably has little to do with lawsuits (since no successful lawsuits have ever been filed against a "Good Samaritan" physician or nurse) and more to do with not being able to render emergency care adequately or not wanting to become involved.

Interestingly, Vermont has legislation that requires physicians to render emergency aid. Its legality or constitutionality has yet to be reviewed by an appellate court, however.

As a nurse volunteering emergency aid at a roadside accident, must I follow police instructions?

The police have the right to order you to terminate treatment or remove the patient, even against medical advice. But the police cannot force you to perform services or dictate how medical care will be carried out.

Can I be liable for free advice?

Yes. In free-advice situations, the same legal rules apply as in other situations where you render advice as part of your professional duties. Therefore, if you volunteer free advice, you can incur liability if the advice is inappropriate and causes damage.

What standard of care do I owe a person to whom I give free health-care advice?

The same degree of care as is owed to a regular patient. Therefore, you should follow the same standards you would employ in responding to a hospital patient. You should try to imagine that an inquiring friend or relative is a complete stranger asking the same question in the hospital. If you find it necessary to give advice, it is wise to document all the circumstances in a dated and signed entry in your personal journal.

Must I comply with my state's nurse practice act when I volunteer my services, say, at a community function?

Most state nurse practice acts do not extend to volunteer services; they specify only the legal limits of paid nursing practice. This also means that a nonlicensed person may provide nursing care without pay and without being subject to the standards of nurse practice acts. This does not mean, however, that you cannot incur liability as a result of negligently performed volunteer standards. In fact, you may have greater potential liability because your legal status is less defined than when you are performing salaried services.

Am I free from professional liability if I provide health-care advice to a friend or relative without accepting compensation for it?

No. The fact that you do not accept compensation does not mean that you have no legal duty to the person who is relying on your advice. For this reason, nurses and other health-care providers should resist offering casual advice, and all health-care providers should check to see whether their malpractice coverage extends to such situations.

What specific guidelines should I follow when volunteering advice to a friend or relative?

Even a casual conversation can create nursing liability. To help minimize the risks, you should observe the following guidelines:

1. Give advice only within the scope of your nurse practice act, education, and experience.
2. Avoid speculation about the illness or prognosis.
3. Never suggest that a friend change or ignore his doctor's orders.
4. Never offer advice that, if wrong, could cause serious or permanent damage.
5. Record any advice you give in your personal nursing log or journal.

Are there any particular risks involved when I do ear piercing, such as when I am employed as part of a jewelry promotion?

Many states have specific statutes or regulations governing ear piercing, and these should first be reviewed.

You should always obtain a release and acknowledgment that ear piercing can cause infection. This protects you from a lawsuit related to infection that results from piercing done according to accepted standards.

You should, of course, refuse to pierce the ears of a minor without a signed parental consent.

Finally, you should check your malpractice insurance for coverage. Most policies consider such activities as ear piercing beyond the scope of conventional nursing services for which you would be insured.

As a registered nurse employed by a hospital, do I have a duty to provide emergency care to a patient not assigned to me?

Yes. An emergency that occurs in the normal hospital setting may call for immediate action on your part to provide care to a patient, even though he may not be assigned to you. This is so because as a general-duty nurse employed by a hospital, you assume a duty of care to all patients for whose benefit your nursing services are engaged. The same may be said for nurses employed by school systems, industrial plants, public health departments, and the like.

As a home-care nurse, may I refuse to provide care to a patient?

Home-care services may be provided only to patients who are cared for by a responsible person. Nurses can, and should, refuse to admit a patient to home-care services if the patient is not safe at home. Once the patient has been accepted, you cannot refuse to provide care, but you must initiate appropriate action if you determine that the patient's safety or health is in jeopardy.

May nurses working in a hospice accept standing orders for pain medication?

Although hospital nurses may follow standing orders for pain, medication nurses working in a hospice should not. As a hospice nurse, you should obtain specific orders signed by your patient's doctor before administering pain medication.

What are the various nursing responsibilities among the different levels of nursing in a geriatric care facility?

There can be considerable fragmentation of nursing care in a geriatric facility.

The RN is responsible for overall patient assessment and evaluation. The LPN or licensed vocational nurse (LVN) decides on the daily assessment, evaluation, and planning. The nurse's aide implements the assessment plan.

This division of responsibility can create confusion and a poorly coordinated approach to patient care, and can cause liability unless the nursing staff properly organizes and performs its work.

Do nurses working in alternative settings face greater legal risks than hospital nurses face?

Possibly. While nurses find that alternative work settings frequently offer greater challenges and professional freedom, they may also represent increased legal risks and additional responsibilities. For instance, if you are a nurse who is working alone, you are working without the support of supervisors, senior nurses, and other health professionals. Moreover, you are without specialized equipment and other hospital resources. And if you are working in a less structured environment, you must rely more on yourself and your own professional judgment than on formal institutional policy.

Can I be judged by different standards if I work in an alternative setting, for example, as a school nurse or a community health nurse?

No. While your nursing duties will necessarily be different from those of a hospital-based nurse, the courts have not applied special standards to nurses who work in alternative settings. Nurse practice acts generally do not describe professional standards for nurses working in various settings. Therefore, if you work in an alternative setting and violate those standards, your license can be suspended or revoked by the state nursing board. It is true, however, that the ANA establishes different standards for different practice areas (e.g., gerontology, community health).

Do nurses in a geriatric facility (or skilled nursing facility) have an obligation to report patient neglect or maltreatment?

The majority of states have passed laws that make reporting maltreatment or neglect of patients mandatory. Most of these states specifically confine this obligation to nursing home rather than hospital situations. Elder abuse legislation is now under consideration in most of the remaining states. Several states have also established liaison or ombudsman offices to investigate abusive situations.

Does a physician's assistant (PA) have the authority to issue orders to me?

This depends on the specific statutory authority granted to PAs within the state. For example, Florida specifically grants PAs this authority. If the statutory authority is unclear, you should decline to follow a PA's orders unless the authority is granted by hospital policy or the orders are countersigned by a supervising physician. Where a PA cannot legally issue orders, however, it would be illegal for you to follow such non-countersigned orders, even if otherwise suggested by hospital policy.

As a private-duty nurse, may I refuse to provide nursing care to a particular patient?

Yes. In contrast to the general-duty hospital nurse, who is normally expected to provide nursing care to any number of hospital patients, as a private-duty nurse you are considered a free agent and may decide for yourself whether you wish to accept employment by any particular person. Your refusal to accept an offer of private employment will not subject you to any legal liability because no nurse–patient relationship has come into being.

As a nurse engaged in a specialized field of nursing, am I held to a higher standard of care than a general-duty nurse?

Yes. When you have acquired the necessary education and training to engage in a specialized field of nursing, such as pediatrics or surgical nursing, you are held to a higher standard of care than the general-duty nurse in carrying out your duties, but only while performing services in your specialty. The standard of care expected of you as a nurse specialist is that you must exercise the degree of care and skill customarily exercised by other nurses who practice that specialty. Here again, we see that the greater your educational background and training, the higher the standard of care the law generally expects of you.

Do industrial nurses face greater risks than nurses with nonindustrial employers?

Industrial nurses generally face a risk of personal liability that exceeds that of other nurses. This is because of the unique interplay between the doctrine of *respondeat superior* (that a master is liable in certain cases for the wrongful acts of his servants) and the laws relating to workmen's compensation.

All state workmen's compensation laws provide that an employer cannot be sued by one of his employees for injury incurred in the course of the employment. As an industrial nurse, your patients would ordinarily be employees of the same organization that employs you. Under these circumstances, when your negligent conduct leads to injury, an injured employee can sue only you.

As a school nurse employed in a state that is immune from tort liability under the doctrine of governmental immunity, do I have the same legal exposure as nurses employed by other branches of the state government?

Yes. In the United States, the rules relating to governmental immunity affect not only nurses employed directly by state governments but also nurses employed by school districts. This is so because education is a state function in the United States, and a school district is therefore legally considered a subdivision of the state government. Accordingly, if you are employed by a school district, you will be subject to the same legal liabilities for tortious conduct as other government employees in that jurisdiction.

6

Liability for the Acts of Others

Malpractice cases seldom involve only one potential defendant. Even when the negligent act may be confined to one individual, the question is invariably asked, Who else may be responsible?

Consider the possibilities. If you are negligent, what is the amount of liability of your employer? Can a unit supervisor be liable for the negligent acts of a subordinate? What is the liability of an attending physician if you perform a wrongful act under the physician's supervision? How about the example of two or more personnel jointly making an error in judgment?

Each question underscores the importance of realizing that you may be liable for other people's negligent performance—and they in turn may be responsible for yours. This chapter discusses the various relationships in nursing in order to define these particular obligations.

What is meant by the term *respondeat superior*?

Respondeat superior is a legal doctrine that holds an employer liable for the negligent acts of his employees that occur while they are carrying out his orders or are otherwise serving his interests. Since most nurses are employed by others, this doctrine assumes a position of great importance and accordingly should be clearly understood.

The doctrine of *respondeat superior* applies (1) only when there is an employer–employee relationship; and (2) only with respect to negligent acts committed within the scope of the employment. The theory behind the doctrine is that an employer should be held legally responsible for the conduct of those persons (employees) whose actions he has a right to direct or control. As you will soon see, the doctrine applies to most, but not all, employers of nurses.

Is the hospital liable under *respondeat superior* for my negligent acts as a private-duty nurse hired and paid by a patient?

The rule of *respondeat superior* does not ordinarily apply when you offer your services as a private-duty nurse, since the relationship thus established is not one of employer–employee. As a private-duty nurse, you are considered an independent contractor and are held legally responsible for your own conduct. This does not apply, however, when you work under the direction, supervision, and control of a hospital or private physician. If you accept a private-duty case, you should have a very clear understanding of who your employer is.

Are there circumstances when a hospital may not be liable for my negligent acts when they occurred within the scope of my employment?

Yes. The first important exception to the *respondeat superior* doctrine can have far-reaching financial consequences for nurses who practice in certain states. In these states, the doctrine of charitable immunity applies, which holds that a charitable (i.e., nonprofit) hospital cannot be sued by a person who has been injured as the result of the negligence of a hospital employee. The practical effect of this rule is to force the injured person to sue the negligent hospital employee personally.

Another exception to the *respondeat superior* doctrine comes into play when the nurse is employed by the state or federal government. The common-law rule of governmental immunity provides that governments cannot be held liable for the negligent acts of their employees while carrying out governmental activities. Some states have changed this rule by statute, however, and in these particcular jurisdictions the doctrine of *respondeat superior* continues to apply to the acts of nurses employed by the state government.

If the hospital that employs me is required to pay damages to an injured patient because of my negligence, can the hospital then recover this amount from me?

Any employer required (under the doctrine of *respondeat superior*) to pay damages to an injured person because of the negligence of his employee has the legal right to recover or be reimbursed that amount from the negligent employee.

As a practical matter, however, very few employers attempt to recover from their employees. One reason is that few employees have sufficient assets to satisfy substantial judgments.

It should be noted carefully that while the doctrine of *respondeat superior* gives the patient someone else to sue, it does not relieve you, as a negligent nurse, from your ultimate liability to the patient. Moreover, any employer required to pay a judgment because of your negligence is less likely to seek reimbursement from you than to terminate your employment. Thus, while *respondeat superior* affords you a certain degree of assurance that your employer will pay the claim, it is not, and should not be thought of as, a shield against liability for acts of malpractice.

If I have committed an act of malpractice, am I held liable even though I am employed by a physician or a hospital?

If there is one rule that all nurses should know and clearly understand, it is the fundamental rule of law that every person is liable for his own tortious conduct. This is called the *rule of personal liability*. The law does not permit a wrongdoer (in the tort-liability sense) to avoid legal liability for his own wrongdoing, even though someone else may also be sued and may be held legally liable for the wrongful conduct in question under another rule of law.

For example, let's assume that you work for a private physician who tells you to execute a medical order that both of you know to be improper. The physician assures you that he will take full responsibility for any harmful consequences. If the patient is harmed and sues you for your conduct, the patient can recover against you. No physician (or any other party) can alter the rule of personal liability by his agreement to assume responsibility. In the final analysis, you will always be held liable for your own negligent conduct.

May a physician ever be liable for my negligence as a nurse?

Yes. The "borrowed-servant" rule holds that an employer is not liable for injury negligently caused by an employee or "servant" if the latter is, at the time, in the special service of another. A supervising physician, rather than the hospital, may be held liable for your negligence as a nurse if you are found to be the physician's borrowed servant or agent because the physician has given you specific instructions or otherwise exercised supervision or control.

Nevertheless, giving instructions to a nurse will not in itself render the physician liable for the nurse's negligence in carrying out those instructions. The determining factor is the right to control and direct the means and methods of the servant's work. A primary example of this is the degree of control exercised by a surgeon over surgical nurses.

Although the doctrine is being subjected to increasing court review, resulting in its modification or abolition in many states, it may still be applied in some cases involving allied health providers.

If I commit a negligent act, is it possible for the physician or hospital to be held liable, while I escape liability?

Since a fundamental rule of law is that every person is liable for his or her own tortious conduct, you would always remain liable, notwithstanding the liability your negligence may impose on the hospital, the physician, or both.

As a nursing supervisor, to what extent can I be held liable for the acts of a subordinate?

As a supervisory nurse, you are not automatically liable for all acts of negligence on the part of those whom you supervise, but you may be held liable when you are negligent in supervising others.

Negligence in supervision is a growing cause of malpractice claims against registered nurses. The RN who is a supervisor, unlike other categories of nurses, is legally and professionally responsible for directing and supervising the activities of practical nurses, nurse's aides, and other nurses involved in direct patient care. Ordinarily, as a supervisor you are held liable only for your own negligence in caring for a patient, but you can also be held liable, under circumstances, for the negligence of someone you are supervising.

Liability for negligence is generally based on (1) failure of the supervisor to determine which of the patient's needs she can safely assign to a subordinate nurse; or (2) failure of the supervisor to give closer personal supervision to a subordinate who requires such supervision.

Can I be held liable for mistakes made by a student nurse under my supervision?

Yes. If you have a responsibility for supervising and instructing a student, you can be held liable for an error resulting from improper supervision.

Ordinarily, you as a staff nurse do not have responsibility for supervising and instructing a student. This responsibility typically rests with a nursing instructor and cannot be delegated. If, however, you volunteer to supervise a student, you can be at risk for the improper acts of the student.

As a nursing supervisor, am I liable if I allow a nurse to perform a treatment or function for which the nurse has inadequate training and experience, and as a result the subordinate causes injury to a patient?

Yes. As a nursing supervisor, you are expected to know whether the one to whom specific nursing duties are assigned is competent to perform those duties, with or without supervision. Your inability to evaluate properly the patient's nursing needs, the nurse's capabilities, or both, will be sufficient to hold you liable for any harm that results to the patient.

The nurse negligently performing the service would also be liable, and the hospital, under the doctrine of *respondeat superior*, would be liable for the negligent acts of both you and the negligent nurse.

Can I be liable for the negligent acts of a volunteer?

Yes. A volunteer should be allowed to perform only those functions he or she is capable of performing. You can be liable for allowing a volunteer to perform services for which he or she is unqualified.

As a nursing instructor, am I liable if a student nurse performs tasks that only a licensed nurse can legally perform?

Yes. Allowing a student nurse to perform unauthorized acts constitutes a breach of duty and imposes liability if there is any resultant injury to the patient.

What is my legal status if I work as a temporary agency nurse?

When you work for an agency, an employer–employee relationship develops, and the agency shares responsibility with you for any negligent acts committed by you within the scope of your duties.

As an agency employee, you may be assigned to work in a patient's home or to care for a patient in a hospital or other health-care institution. These different practice settings may influence how a court will view the agency relationship. For example, by working as supplemental hospital staff, you may impose liability on the hospital under the "borrowed servant" doctrine insofar as the hospital is in a position to control your actions. When the courts interpret this degree of control to exist, the legal liability shifts from the agency to the hospital or institution.

Are there guidelines outlining the responsibilities of temporary nursing agencies and agency nurses?

Yes. The ANA has issued guidelines saying that an agency has a duty to select, orient, evaluate, and assign nurses, and to provide them with professional development.

Agency nurses, according to these same guidelines, should keep their licenses current, select reputable employees, maintain their nursing skills, observe the standards of practice, document their nursing practice, and adhere to the policies and procedures of their agencies.

Does a hospital or institution have any special obligations to agency nurses?

Yes. The hospital or institution is obligated to supply sufficient equipment for proper patient care and to keep its premises and equipment in safe condition. The institution must also familiarize agency nurses with the institution's policies and procedures, and orient these nurses to the same extent as employees of the hospital.

What special responsibilities does a temporary nursing agency have when providing temporary nursing care?

The ANA has issued guidelines outlining responsibilities for temporary nursing agencies and agency nurses. These guidelines require agencies adequately to select, orient, evaluate, and assign nurses, and to provide them with professional development.

Agency nurses, according to these guidelines, should do the following:

- Select reputable agencies.
- Keep their licenses current.
- Maintain nursing skills.
- Observe standards of professional practice.
- Document their nursing practice.
- Adhere to the policies of their agency and clients.

If a hospital were to engage my services as a private-duty or temporary agency nurse for general-duty nursing over a weekend, would the hospital be liable under *respondeat superior* for my negligent acts?

The legal responsibilities in such a situation are the same as if you were a full-time staff nurse at the hospital. *Remember*: The doctrine of *respondeat superior* is tied to the nurse's employment status at the time of the malpractice, not the employment status she usually enjoys. If you were employed by the hospital at the time of the negligent act, the hospital would share liability.

Is a hospital liable for my negligent acts as a private-duty nurse?

Generally speaking, as a private-duty nurse (one who offers her services on behalf of a specific patient), you are working as an independent contractor. The legal effect of this method of employment is that you are solely responsible for all professional services rendered, and the person who has engaged your services can look to you alone for legal satisfaction in the event of an act of malpractice. Personal legal liability attaches to your negligent acts as a private-duty nurse—regardless of the manner in which you were engaged—under the legal theory that no other person or legal entity has the right to direct or control your activities.

Perhaps even more important, no one else (aside from the patient or one acting on behalf of the patient) has the right to discharge you. As a private-duty nurse engaged by a hospitalized patient, you may be subject to the hospital's administrative rules, but you are in all other respects independent of the hospital in carrying out your professional duties.

Does a hospital have any obligation to supervise me if I am working as a private-duty nurse employed by the patient?

Although a hospital is not usually held liable for your negligent acts as a private-duty nurse, an increasing number of cases hold that a hospital has the obligation to provide some supervisory control. Hospital controls include checking private-duty nurse credentials and approving qualifications. The hospital also has the right to insist that you comply with the hospital's policies and procedures.

The JCAH standards and those of other accrediting agencies require nurses from temporary nursing-care agencies to have the same orientation as do regular staff nurses.

As a supervisory nurse, do I have an obligation toward a private-duty nurse?

It is your responsibility as a supervisory nurse to provide the private-duty nurse with such support and assistance as is reasonably required to fulfill the hospital's primary obligation to the patient. The hospital nursing staff must remember that although the private-duty nurse is caring for one of her own patients, the hospital has a continuing obligation toward the patient as well.

7

Liability from Unauthorized Treatment

One of the more serious problems constantly faced by nurses involves claims by patients of wrongfully rendered treatment without the permission of the patient. Without proper consent, a patient can start a suit for assault and battery.

Most laypeople think the term *assault and battery* means striking a person or causing a person bodily injury through physical means. Admittedly this is one common application of the term, but it can also apply to a health practitioner providing life-sustaining treatment to a patient when the patient does not agree to it. It is a well-recognized principle of law that all persons have the right to decide whether to accept or reject treatment.

Within a medicolegal context, nurses must take the necessary precautions to make sure that the patient accepts treatment and that the consent is valid. Of greater concern is the question of the procedures to be followed when consent is refused, even when the consent is necessary to preserve the health of the patient.

Nurses must follow specific guidelines if they are effectively to handle the consent problems associated with intoxicated persons, minors, mentally handicapped patients, comatose individuals, and other patients who either refuse treatment or throw into question their ability to consent. This chapter outlines the proper liability-reducing procedures.

Can I be held liable for performing procedures on a patient whose informed consent has not been obtained?

Although the primary responsibility for obtaining informed consent rests with the physician, you can also be held liable when you either knew or should have known that informed consent was not obtained. In these situations, you may share liability with the hospital, physician, and other health providers participating in the unauthorized procedure.

What procedure should be followed when a patient refuses consent to treatment?

When a patient refuses treatment, the physician has a responsibility to explain the risks involved in refusing treatment. This can also be your responsibility as a nurse when the patient refuses continued treatment.

In these circumstances, you should notify your supervisor and the patient's physician, and record the patient's refusal in your notes.

Next, the patient should be asked to sign a refusal-of-treatment release. If the patient refuses to sign, the continued refusal should be witnessed by one or two individuals, and the incident should again be recorded in your notes.

For added protection, most hospitals also attempt to have the patient's spouse or other close relative sign the refusal-of-treatment release.

What is the hospital's duty when a patient refuses a specific treatment?

It is the obligation of the hospital, in the face of a patient's refusal, to make sure that no member of the hospital staff performs the refused procedure. If the hospital does not successfully prevent unauthorized procedures, it may be legally liable to the patient to the same extent as the doctor or nurse who performed the procedure.

The hospital is also legally obligated to continue to render the best medical care possible within the limitations imposed by the patient's refusal. While a patient may refuse to consent to any treatment, it has been said by one court that the patient cannot "demand mistreatment." Only if a patient consistently refuses to participate in any treatment program might the hospital, after making diligent attempts verbally to persuade the patient to change his mind, be justified in asking the patient to leave.

Can a patient waive his right to medical information before consenting to surgical or medical treatment?

Yes. A patient's rights to be informed include his right *not* to be informed. If the patient indicates to his doctor that he doesn't want to know the details of treatment, the doctor has two responsibilities: (1) The doctor must make the patient aware that there are risks and alternatives; (2) the doctor should obtain from the patient express and explicit waiver of disclosure.

What are the rights of minors to consent on their own to medical care?

A minor (usually under the age of 18) has the right to consent to treatment for sexually transmitted diseases, serious communicable diseases, and drug and alcohol abuse.

A mature minor (i.e., a minor whom a doctor or iudge might consider mature) has the right to consent to or refuse medical experimentation, routine care, and emergency care. Mature minors can also obtain contraceptives and abortion (although their parents may have to be notified), and can request a second opinion if their parents have them mentally committed.

Do any laws specifically require informed consent?

Many states have passed laws that endorse the requirements of informed consent as set by the courts. Several of these states define informed consent or specify the claims and defenses that can be made in informed-consent cases.

Other states have procedural laws on informed consent. For example, a state may specify possible defenses to a claim based on nonconsent.

Still other states have laws on consent but not on *informed* consent.

Have any states passed specific laws requiring informed consent to treatment?

Yes. At least 12 states have passed substantive laws that define informed consent or specify the claims and defenses that can be made in informed-consent cases.

Other states have procedural laws that specify how informed consent is to be obtained. Still other states have laws limited to the legal effect of documents such as consent forms.

What is the purpose of a written consent form?

The consent of the patient is put into writing for the same reason that most contracts are put into writing: to preserve the exact terms of the consent in case of future disagreement. For example, should a patient sue a doctor or a hospital and allege lack of informed consent, the doctor can present the written consent form in court as evidence that consent was in fact obtained. If the form is specific on its terms, and was voluntarily signed by a competent and understanding patient, the patient has very little chance of winning a lawsuit.

Under what conditions must the doctor or hospital obtain the patient's informed consent?

The general rule is that any time there is an inherent risk of death or serious bodily injury that the patient might not know about, or when the probability of success in a medical procedure is low, the person performing the test or treatment is required to obtain the patient's informed consent. The rule applies equally to administration of investigational use drugs, the performance of diagnostic tests, and the performance of major or minor surgical procedures. An example of a procedure that probably does not require that specific disclosures be made because the risks are both minimal and generally known is the taking of a blood sample. Conversely, diagnostic tests such as angiograms and myelograms do require informed consent.

Who is responsible for obtaining informed consent?

The primary responsibility rests with the physician; he or she is the one who will carry out the treatment or procedure. As a nurse, you should not participate in any treatment or procedure if there is reason to believe informed consent was not obtained. A court may find you liable, together with the physician, for performing a nonconsensual treatment when you had reason to suspect the procedure was undertaken without consent.

How is consent obtained?

Consent may be obtained verbally or in writing, or it can be implied by the actions of the patient. In the hospital setting, consent has traditionally been obtained through the use of blanket consent forms.

Such forms technically meet the consent requirement. But these broad forms are frequently so vague and broadly worded as to give the patient almost no information about what he is consenting to. For this reason, these forms should not be used; indeed, they are generally found legally ineffectual by the courts. Because of the use of vague forms and the lack of communication of more detailed information about treatment to patients, the courts recognize the need for informed consent if consent is to be valid.

Is it essential that a patient sign a consent form?

Few states require written consent, but it certainly is sound practice to insist on it. Of equal importance is that a physician have a witness present as he verbally explains risks and procedures to a patient.

Some states accept as evidence of informed consent a physician's handwritten clinical notes stating that he discussed the proposed procedure, its risks, benefits, and alternatives, with the patient.

Is a signed consent form conclusive evidence that the patient issued informed consent?

No. A signed consent form may be evidence of informed consent, but in itself it is not conclusive. Even if a patient signs a consent form, he may still challenge the validity of consent in court. For example, the patient may argue that he did not understand the information or did not receive sufficient information. For this reason, it is helpful to have a third party witness the extent of disclosure and the information provided to the patient.

Can legal consent be given without signing a consent form?

Yes. As noted previously, the reason for a writing is only to maintain a permanent record of what was agreed to. No writing is required to make most contracts, and no written form is required to make consent to treatment valid. Consent may also be implied by actions, such as the voluntary submission to treatment.

Obviously, the hospital should require a well-documented written consent for any surgery or unusual treatment to prevent the patient from later denying the existence of consent.

What is a "blanket" consent form?

A blanket consent form is one that covers almost everything a doctor or a hospital might do to a patient, without mentioning any specific treatment. Many hospitals continue to require patients to sign such forms on admission. A typical form reads: "I, the undersigned, hereby grant permission for the administration of any anesthetic to, and for the performance of any operation upon myself as may be deemed advisable by the surgeon in attendance at the hospital."

The general rule is that a blanket consent form is almost always legally inadequate. Usually, the more vague and indefinite the terms of the consent, the more specifically the form will be construed by a court against the doctor or the hospital.

If a patient signs a consent form, can he then challenge the validity of his consent?

In most states, a signed consent form is evidence of informed consent, but it is not conclusive evidence. The patient can always argue that he did not understand the information or that the information was inadequate for the consent to be informed.

Are there enforceable clauses in consent forms by which the patient agrees not to sue the hospital or doctors?

The general answer is that a patient cannot legally waive his right to sue a hospital or doctor in the event of malpractice. Such agreements have consistently been held unenforceable as being against public policy. For this reason, few hospitals continue to use these forms. Nevertheless, there remain hospitals and physicians that believe the value of such waivers is to cause patients to think they have lost their right to sue.

These waivers should not be confused with a patient releasing the hospital or physician after an act of malpractice occurs. The latter, of course, are enforceable if a patient knowingly and willfully discharges an existing claim.

What should I do if a physician refuses to obtain informed consent?

You should refuse to participate in the procedure and should inform your supervisor of your reasons for not participating.

Is patient consent valid if given under the influence of a drug?

For consent to be valid, it must be given voluntarily, competently, and with knowledge of all relevant facts. If the patient is under the influence of a drug that compromises any of these components of consent, the consent is probably not valid.

Particular care should be used when obtaining consent from a patient on mind-altering drug therapy. The patient should be carefully questioned to determine whether he actually understands the issues, and the patient's condition should, wherever possible, be observed by a witness. In addition, there should be appropriate notes and observations in the patient's charts.

What procedures should I follow in obtaining consent from a sedated patient?

If you know in advance that a physician will require consent from a sedated patient, you should inform the physician of the patient's medication schedule so that the physician may arrange a time to obtain the consent when the patient is competent to make a judgment.

How can a physician obtain consent from a comatose patient?

If the patient is comatose from a long-term condition, the physician (through the hospital) should ask the court to appoint a conservator or guardian. But if immediate treatment is needed, the physician may properly obtain consent from a near relative or even the hospital administrator if time does not permit family consent.

These same procedures should also be followed with a minor or incompetent patient.

What is the significance of my witnessing a consent form?

Your signature as a witness signifies that you saw the patient sign the consent form and that the patient appeared to be aware of what he signed. A recommended procedure is to have the patient read the completed consent form, and for you to check the patient's chart to be sure that the patient is not taking depressants or other mind-altering drugs.

Many hospitals have a policy of requiring a nurse to witness a consent form. This supports the physician's claim that he followed proper procedure in obtaining consent. If this is the purpose of your action, then it is necessary that you actually be present when the physician explains the procedure.

Do nurses and allied health professionals have a right to refuse to witness informed-consent forms?

Yes. Acting as a witness to legal documents is not part of the delivery of health care that nurses and allied health-care professionals are legally obligated to render. Nevertheless, these health professionals may feel considerable pressure to sign consent forms as witness. In such cases, they should observe the entire consent process and sign only if they agree that fully informed consent has been obtained. If they are unable to do this, for any reason, and still feel that they are not free to refuse to sign the form, they should add after their signature a notation such as "witness to the signature only." This will help clarify their role to all concerned.

Should I witness an authorization or informed-consent form when I shall be involved in the treatment?

No. When you are to be a party to a planned medical procedure, you should not act as a witness. Many state nurse practice acts specifically prohibit a nurse from acting as a witness under these situations.

Does the amount of information that must be disclosed to obtain informed consent depend on the elective nature of the procedure?

One can summarize the informed-consent cases by noting that the key element is self-determination and the desire to give the patient enough information so that the patient can decide how and if he is to be treated. A corollary is that the more elective a procedure is, the more important full disclosure becomes. If there is only one treatment available, and death is imminent, the rationale behind informed consent is less compelling.

Should consent be obtained for the administration of drugs or the use of nonsurgical procedure?

The theory behind informed consent does not apply only to surgical procedures. Any time a patient is subjected to a risk that would be deemed "material," informed consent should be obtained. For example, the American Heart Association, in one of its publications, includes a proposed consent form for exercise testing.

If a drug puts a patient at risk, the patient should be so informed. An obvious example would be telling a long-distance truck driver that a particular medication might make him drowsy. In one case, a court recently ruled that it was a question for the jury to decide whether or not the manufacturer of Anacin had satisfactorily warned the public of the dangers of prolonged use of the drug by stating that if pain persisted for more than ten days, the user should consult a physician. A corollary to this rule requires drug companies to inform physicians fully of adverse side effects of their products.

For many common nursing procedures, consent is implied. It is neither appropriate nor necessary to obtain a specific written patient consent for such procedures as enemas, urinary catheterization, or the insertion of a nasogastric tube, for example. The standard of practice would include a thorough explanation of the procedures and the expected benefits to the patient.

Is the consent of a family member necessary when the patient is a competent adult?

No. This is so even when the family member has a direct interest in the procedure. This question most often arises when the family member is the spouse. In one case, a physician performed a successful hysterectomy on his patient. The patient's husband sued the physician, alleging that he interfered with his "marital rights." Before the surgery, the husband had notified the physician that he "strenuously objected" to the performance of the surgery. The court held that the consent of the husband was unnecessary and that he had no right to a "childbearing wife."

Can a doctor determine that a patient is incompetent?

Yes. The facts indicating that a patient is or is not competent are available to physicians, and physicians are capable of making determinations that a patient is confused or appears not to comprehend what is being said to him. Only a court, however, may legally determine a person to be legally incompetent, and may authorize another person (usually a guardian or conservator) to consent to the treatment of the incompetent patient.

Is the husband's consent legally necessary for any medical treatment of a married woman?

The consent of a husband is never legally necessary for the treatment of a conscious, competent, and consenting married woman. This has been consistently affirmed by the courts. Specific cases considered in the context of a husband suing the doctor for treating his wife without his consent have included both sterilization and pregnancy care. The husband's consent was determined not to be necessary even in these instances. These findings, of course, work both ways; the wife's consent is not required for any medical treatment of her husband.

As a matter of policy, hospitals and physicians may request spousal consent, particularly if the operation involves sterilization, but such consent is not required in the strict legal sense.

When is a doctor justified in not disclosing the risks and material facts concerning a recommended treatment to a patient?

Since the major rationale for the doctrine of informed consent is the preservation and protection of individual self-determination, the exceptions to the rule should involve only those cases in which self-determination is impossible. Typical of such cases are minors (whose parents may usually make legally valid decisions concerning their treatment), unconscious patients in emergency situations, and patients found to be mentally incompetent to make decisions about their own health care.

Is a blood test, such as a blood alcohol test, admissible in court if the person refused consent to the test?

Legal opinions continue to differ, but a recent Supreme Court decision held that a blood extraction obtained without a warrant but incident to lawful arrest is not an unconstitutional search and seizure, and is therefore admissible evidence.

Courts have also admitted blood tests as evidence when the tests were not drawn at police request but for medically necessary purposes such as blood typing.

Still other states have held that a person implies his consent to submit to a blood test if he is arrested for driving under the influence of alcohol.

What steps should be followed when a patient refuses to grant consent to treatment that the physician believes is necessary?

The physician has an obligation to inform the patient of the risks of refusing treatment. This disclosure must be as complete as the disclosure necessary to obtain consent.

Many hospitals require patients to sign a waiver-of-treatment form when consent is refused, and documenting the refusal should be as thorough as in obtaining informed consent. In summary, nonconsent must be on as informed a basis as consent.

Under what circumstances may a court overrule a patient's right to refuse treatment?

The obvious basis to challenge a patient's refusal is when a patient is mentally incompetent to make the decision, and treatment is necessary to preserve life or avoid serious harm.

Other common grounds for overruling a patient's refusal of treatment include the following:

- When refusing treatment endangers the life or health of another

- When a spouse or relative wants to withhold consent on behalf of a comatose or incompetent patient, but the relative has not been appointed legal guardian
- When public interest outweighs the patient's rights, as in mandatory AIDS testing

Can the mere fact that a patient refuses needed treatment be, in itself, evidence of mental incompetency?

No. The refusal itself, no matter how serious the patient's condition, is not evidence of incompetence.

If a hospital attempts to convince a court of a patient's mental incompetency, other tests must be employed. Some of that proof can come from observations of the patient's conduct while in the hospital or prior history of mental illness.

Can a patient refuse emergency life-sustaining treatment?

A competent adult has an absolute right to refuse emergency treatment. This decision cannot be overruled by others unless it can be shown the patient was so badly traumatized by the injury that he was temporarily incompetent. This determination, however, requires careful assessment by the physician, nurse, or emergency medical technician (EMT).

Does a prisoner have the right to refuse lifesaving treatment?

Although competent adults are allowed to reject lifesaving treatment, it appears that prisoners do not share this same right.

Several court decisions suggest that although a prisoner has a constitutional right to privacy, there are limitations on this right, and the state instead has the right to force needed treatment to preserve a prisoner's life.

What would be the best way for me, as a nurse, to cope with a patient's apprehension or unwillingness toward a necessary treatment?

Since most patients react strongly to threats (real or implied) to their individuality, maturity, and adulthood, any procedure that requires them to be submissive is bound to give rise to feelings of helplessness, anxiety, and (to differing degrees) antagonism. In contrast, when the patient is adequately informed of the procedure and encouraged to participate in it, his feelings of helplessness diminish, and he becomes a willing and cooperative partner in the therapeutic relationship.

By definition, patient-centered treatment focuses on the patient rather than on the task, and this personal approach is calculated to be more beneficial both to the patient and to you as a nurse.

Patients should also be encouraged to participate in their care to the greatest extent practicable, thereby creating a more therapeutic relationship between patient and nurse.

Finally, you should consciously try to develop effective interpersonal relationships with your patients and should demonstrate by your words and actions that you not only care for but care about your patients. In the final analysis, however, if a patient refuses treatment despite your best efforts, you must respect and support the patient's decision, and report it as soon as possible to the patient's physician.

Can a patient withdraw consent once it has been granted?

Yes. A patient always has the right to withdraw or terminate consent. When this occurs, the physician should terminate treatment in a way least likely to cause injury to the patient and should inform the patient of the risks associated with interrupted treatment.

When does a patient's informed consent become invalid?

Informed consent can be considered invalid if a change in the patient's medical status alters the risks and benefits of treatment he originally consented to. In such a case, the physician must inform the patient of any new risks, benefits, or alternatives appropriate to the patient's changed condition.

Can I physically restrain a patient who refuses to accept treatment?

No. You cannot legally restrain a competent patient simply to enforce treatment on someone who refuses to follow orders. To do so would make you liable for assault and battery and false imprisonment.

When parents are divorced, which parent has the authority to grant consent on behalf of a child?

Generally, the parent with legal custody has the legal right to grant consent. If the parents share legal custody, then either parent can grant consent.

The courts, however, increasingly recognize the rights of a noncustodial parent to issue consent, particularly when the custodial parent is unavailable or arbitrarily and without good cause denies consent to needed medical care on behalf of the child.

Is a minor's consent to treatment legally valid?

Not usually. Since a minor's consent to treatment is legally invalid, the physician must obtain substitute consent from a parent or legal guardian. In these cases, the physician must disclose to the parents or guardian all relevant information to ensure that the consent is informed. When emergency treatment is required to avoid serious consequences, the law imposes implied consent, allowing such treatment as is necessary until valid consent can be obtained.

Can a minor ever decide for himself whether to accept or refuse treatment?

A minor's rights in making independent decisions about medical treatment are more restricted than an adult's rights. Nevertheless, in some cases a court may decide a minor is sufficiently mature to decide for himself whether to accept or reject treatment. In these situations, the minor, not the parents, has the decision-making authority, although in practice consent is often sought from minors who are approaching the age of consent.

Under what circumstances may a court appoint a guardian *ad litem* to oversee the interests of a minor?

Whenever the court determines that a "diversion of interest" exists between the minor and one or both of his parents, a guardian may be appointed. A guardian has full authority to make decisions on behalf of the child. An example of this may be when the parents seek to impose their religious beliefs on the child and thus prevent the child from obtaining needed medical care.

Of course, a court will also appoint a guardian for a minor who is without a parent.

Can a minor be treated for sexually transmitted or other communicable diseases without parental consent?

Most states (and Canadian provinces) have laws that permit minors to consent to treatment for serious communicable and sexually transmitted diseases without parental knowledge or consent. This would normally include the right to be tested and treated for AIDS.

What should a hospital do when a minor needs emergency care, but parental consent cannot be immediately obtained?

The general rule is to treat first and obtain consent later. Under these circumstances, the law "implies" consent, and, of course, it is also the most defensible position because it prevents further injury. The hospital should, however, notify the parents and obtain consent for further treatment as soon as possible.

May minors legally be given contraceptive devices without their parents' consent?

Yes. Recent Supreme Court rulings have held that a state may not prohibit the distribution or use of contraceptives by minors—whether married or unmarried. The Court found that the constitutional right to privacy applies to minors, and since states cannot outlaw abortions for minors, or even require parental consent for a minor to obtain an abortion, the Court reasoned it would make no sense to permit the state to outlaw the sale of contraceptives to minors. Although previous cases dealt specifically with nonprescription contraceptives, the Court's reasoning would likely be equally applicable to prescription contraceptives.

Does a minor require parental consent for substance-abuse treatment?

No. State and federal laws allow minors to consent to substance-abuse treatment and rehabilitation programs without parental consent.

Moreover, like adults, minor children in drug treatment programs are entitled to have their records sealed and kept confidential.

Can a parent commit a minor child to a mental health facility against the consent of the minor?

A nonconsenting minor can be admitted to a mental health facility at the request of either or both parents.

Such minors, however, have the right to have a psychiatrist make an independent finding of their condition and medical need, both before admission and at least once thereafter.

Some states follow more rigid admission policies, including the minor's right to a hearing and representation by counsel either before or shortly after admission.

May I treat an emancipated minor without parental consent?

Yes. An emancipated minor is one who is no longer under the care, custody, and control of his parents. Thus, a married minor or one who is in the armed forces is always considered to be emancipated from his parents, as are mothers of any age. It can be generally said that a minor who is living apart from his parents and is self-supporting is emancipated for the purpose of consenting to medical care. Some states have codified the emancipated-minor rule. In Massachusetts, for example, a minor who is living apart from his parents or guardian and is "managing" his own financial affairs may consent to medical treatment by statute, with certain exceptions.

It is particularly important that nurses practicing in the specialty areas of pediatrics, obstetrics, and emergency care have current information on state statutes concerning the emancipation of minors.

Can an adolescent minor seek a court review of protested or forced hospitalization?

Yes. In such situations, all states allow a minor to obtain a court review and be represented by independent or court-appointed counsel. The court may also appoint an independent guardian in such instances.

Who has legal responsibility for a mentally ill or developmentally disabled patient?

If the patient is a child, the parents or legal guardian are responsible.

If the child has been institutionalized before entering the hospital, the prior institution may have responsibility, particularly if it referred the patient for further treatment.

Should the courts find the parent unqualified or unwilling to care for the child, the court will appoint a legal guardian. This is true of mentally ill adults who may also require guardians.

In most instances, a mentally ill adult will have a spouse, parent, or adult child capable of granting consent on his behalf. If the patient is without a family, the patient should be represented by a guardian or conservator before nonemergency medical care is administered.

What should I do when a mentally ill patient and his guardian are in disagreement about a patient's care?

When there is conflict in the issuance of consent, you should notify your supervisor and the patient's physician, as the situation should be reviewed by the attorneys for the hospital. Often the hospital will seek a court order clarifying the procedure to be followed.

This same advice would also follow when parents are in disagreement over care for a child, or when disagreement exists between two adult children concerning care for an elderly parent.

What procedure should be followed when a doctor or nurse doubts a patient's capacity to consent, even though the patient hasn't been judged legally incompetent?

In this situation, the consent must be obtained from the nearest relative; if none can be found, the court must authorize treatment or appoint a conservator who can make medical decisions on behalf of the patient.

Under what circumstances will a court authorize treatment for an incompetent patient when a spouse or other near relative refuses consent to a needed medical procedure?

The courts often overrule a spouse's or relative's judgment in such cases. Essentially the courts must consider what will happen to the patient if treatment is denied, in contrast to the risks associated with treatment. In cases where the court believes withholding consent is unreasonable and clearly against the best interests of the patient, it will intervene with its own authorization.

Can the state compel the sterilization of a mentally ill or mentally incompetent individual?

Although this issue has not been reviewed by the U.S. Supreme Court for over 50 years, earlier decisions and many lower-court cases seem to uphold the validity of state-enforced sterilization in the following instances:

- When the sterilization is not used as punishment
- When the policy and criteria are equally applied to others
- When the unborn child's interest is sufficient to warrant the sterilization

Usually, the patient's guardian must consent to the procedure, and most states require a presterilization review of the case by a court or administrative agency.

8

Recordkeeping Requirements

In recent years, nursing responsibility for good recordkeeping has grown enormously.

The importance of proper recordkeeping can be seen when we consider the medical record in the following ways:

1. As a basis for planning patient care and for continuity in the evaluation of the patient's condition and treatment
2. As documentary evidence of the course of the patient's medical evaluation, treatment, and change in condition
3. As documentary evidence of communication between the responsible practitioner and any other health professional contributing to the patient's care
4. As protection of the legal interests of the patient, hospital, and practitioner.

With growing governmental involvement in financing and auditing medical care, the purposes of the medical record are likely to continue to expand.

This chapter discusses the major legal issues that surround the making, maintenance, storage, and disposal of nursing records. The issue of patient access is also dealt with, while issues of "privacy" and third-party access to medical records are addressed in Chapter 9.

What is the legal significance of the medical record?

The medical record is often the best evidence of the quality of medical and nursing care, and is significant in establishing the appropriateness of care provided a patient.

What information should I document?

You are required to record accurately, completely, and in a timely manner the following:

- Physician orders that were carried out
- Therapeutic measures, patient education, and treatment that you and other health-care providers perform
- The patient's general and clinical responses to treatment
- The patient's health-related behavior including verbal communication and physical and physiological reactions

What documents are considered to be the patient's medical record for legal purposes?

Each patient's medical record consists of a variety of separate records, including the following:

- Patient admission sheet
- Patient history
- Patient medication record
- Physician's order sheet
- Progress notes
- Nursing-care plan
- Nurse's notes

- Laboratory test results
- X-rays and reports
- Flow sheets
- Discharge summary
- Home-care instruction sheet

What is the legal significance of *not* documenting patient care?

The basic rule in court is that documentation means *done,* and no documentation means *not done.*

While you as a nurse may argue to the contrary, a court is justified in reaching this conclusion when the medical record is silent as to care that was supposedly provided.

Can the failure to document be used against me in a malpractice case?

Yes. There have been many cases where courts inferred that a nurse's failure to document care meant either that she did not perform a required act or that the act was performed improperly. At the least, a failure to document can be viewed as careless conduct, which may be indicative of how services were provided.

Can nursing records be used as evidence in a malpractice case?

Yes, providing the records were kept in the ordinary or usual routine. This then imposes a duty on nurses to maintain records properly and accurately with the understanding that they may someday be examined in court should a malpractice case result. The nursing record is frequently the most important evidence in such a case.

What should I do when a patient demands to see his medical records?

A patient's request should alert you to probe the reasons for the request. If it appears that the patient has anxiety or concern over his treatment, you should contact your supervisor. The supervisor, in turn, should notify the risk manager or the hospital's legal counsel.

You should always remain with the patient while the records are under review, both to respond to any questions the patient may have and to protect the records from alteration or destruction.

What should I, the hospital, or another health provider do if a third party requests copies of a patient's records?

You (or any other health provider) should decline unless you have the prior written consent of the patient. The only exception to this would be where records are asked for under a valid subpoena or are used by other members of the health-care team treating the patient, and the records are needed to coordinate care.

It is particularly important to remember that the children of an elderly patient have no right to information contained in the record of their parent unless permission has been obtained from the patient to disclose specific information.

Is a patient's relative entitled to see the patient's records?

A relative can legally see a patient's records only under one of three conditions:

1. The patient granted approval.
2. The relative is the patient's legal guardian.
3. Circumstances indicate that the patient involves the relative in medical decisions and therefore consent is implied.

In all other situations, you should refuse disclosure until patient consent is obtained. Further, a decision to let a relative see a patient's records should never be made solely by you as a nurse. The patient's physician, your supervisor, or both should also be involved.

What procedures can I follow to reduce liability related to documentation?

There are many ways poor documentation techniques can cause legal difficulties. Any nurse can substantially reduce the chance of error by following these twelve tips:

1. Record the patient's name and identification number on every page of the chart.
2. Record the date and time of each entry.
3. Avoid vague observations or general terms. Be specific.
4. Use standard abbreviations only as prescribed by hospital procedure.
5. Document any nursing action taken in response to a patient's problem.

6. Document the patient's response to treatment and medication.
7. Document procedures and actions after they are performed—never before.
8. Chart an omission as a new entry. Do not backdate or add to previously written entries.
9. Document all safeguards and steps taken to protect a patient.
10. Document incidents in both the progress report and the incident report.
11. Write on each line. Avoid blank spaces that may allow others to insert notes.
12. Document care personally provided. Never document for someone else.

Do any laws protect the privacy of a patient's medical records?

The Federal Privacy Act of 1974 protects confidential medical information of patients in Veterans Administration (VA) hospitals. Several states have also enacted statutes or regulations safeguarding the patient's right to privacy.

But it is primarily the common-law principle that a patient has a right to confidentiality that protects the patient from unwarranted disclosure to third parties.

What rules govern documentation procedures?

The federal government regulates recordkeeping under Medicare and Medicaid. While these regulations must be observed only for participation in these two programs, they are nevertheless important to most hospitals.

The states may have general statutes or regulations on documentation, however. These are usually contained in the state's nurse practice act.

Two professional organizations have set more stringent standards than typically required by state regulation. The ANA establishes standards for documentation in its Standards of Nursing Practice.

The JCAH has standards requiring documentation of each phase of nursing care from patient admission through discharge.

Although the policy of every hospital must necessarily incorporate each of these standards, many hospitals have even more rigorous standards, which must be observed.

Are there special laws concerning the maintenance of psychiatric records?

Yes, often. Some hospitals keep psychiatric records separately, and some state statutes provide that such records be less accessible than other medical records. Psychiatric records are generally viewed, both by the law and by the medical profession, as being more sensitive than general medical records, to the extent that, in some states, patients may be legally barred from viewing their own records.

In many states, statutes require that hospitals or mental institutions make special efforts to keep this information from getting into the hands of unauthorized persons. If you are a nurse handling psychiatric records, you should know both the law of your state and the practice of the hospital involved.

How long should medical and nursing records be maintained?

Because a malpractice case may possibly be commenced many years later, it is a good idea to retain medical records permanently.

Some states specify a minimum time period for record retention; other states have adopted the Uniform Business Records Act, which calls for keeping records for no less than 3 years. Other statutes specify recordkeeping requirements (e.g., for Medicare) that require record retention for 5 years.

Microfilm copies are generally accepted as substitutes for originals, and hospitals routinely store permanent records on microfilm and in electronic form.

Are there situations where a patient impliedly grants consent to disclosure of medical information?

Yes. The first is the implied right to share information with other members of the patient's health-care team.

Then the patient impliedly consents to disclosing such information as is reasonably necessary to bill a third-party payment plan, such as Medicare or Blue Cross.

What is meant by *problem-oriented* records?

With this recordkeeping system, all members of the health-care team, and even the patient, consolidate their information in a format that goes by the acronym SOAP. Each record combines Subjective data (how the patient feels), Objective data (what the nurse observes), Assessment data, and Plans.

SOAP recordkeeping provides a comprehensive and coordinated picture of patient progress; for that reason, it is often preferred over the more conventional source-oriented records. Problem-oriented charting utilizes a list of problems. As each problem is discussed in the chart, the SOAP format is used.

What procedure should I follow if the nurse on the previous shift left blank spaces on the patient's chart?

The best procedure is to draw lines through the blank spaces so that no one can later add information that may be either incorrect or detrimental to the patient or the nursing staff.

If the previous nurse forgot to sign her name to the chart, you as the incoming nurse should begin the entry with the time and date, and a statement as to when your shift began. Then you should sign your name.

What is the correct way for me to sign my notes?

You should sign your notes with your first initial, full last name, and title. The signature should be placed on the right side of the page as proof that you entered all the information between the previous nurse's signature and your own.

What should I do if the previous entry was left unsigned by another nurse?

If the last entry was unsigned, the nurse who made the entry should be contacted and reminded to sign it. If the nurse cannot be reached, you should make a notation in the record to distinguish her entry from later entries.

How should I correct a charting error?

You should draw one line through the error, label it "charting error," and initial it. You should never erase or obliterate an error so that it appears an attempt was made to conceal the error.

What is the legal significance of an RN countersigning notes made by LPNs?

Since this is usually unspecified by a state's nurse practice act, the hospital policy should specify the significance.

One interpretation is that the LPN actually performed the service in the presence of the RN, who directly observed it.

Alternatively, a countersignature may mean that the RN did not personally observe the LPN but that the RN verified the patient-care procedures were performed.

What charting procedure should I follow when I sign a chart on behalf of an aide or orderly who may have performed routine patient care?

You should sign both your name and the aide's name. You should also add a statement that you did not personally observe the patient or patient care and therefore cannot attest to the accuracy of the information.

This disclaimer should, of course, be used whenever you sign a chart containing information you cannot personally verify.

What should I do if another nurse requests that I document her care or sign her notes?

Unless hospital policy requires one nurse to witness another nurse's notes, you should refuse. A countersignature can make you responsible for what is contained in the notes.

Which is safer legally: block charting or time charting?

With block charting, you note the procedures carried out during a particular block of time (i.e., 4 P.M. to 8 P.M.). Block charting may encourage you to summarize patient-care information, but it may discourage you from including all the significant information.

Because of the danger of omitting vital information, block charting isn't as safe as time charting, which encourages nurses to document patient care fully on an hour-by-hour basis.

Are there any special precautions I should take in using flow sheets?

Flow sheets are useful for recording information about routine tasks such as administering medication.

Despite their usefulness, flow sheets can cause a common legal problem. You may treat the flow sheet too casually and neglect to be as accurate in your flow-sheet documentation as you are in recordings on the nurse's notes. This obviously creates an inconsistency between the records that may later prove damaging in a lawsuit.

What is the most common error nurses make when they chart?

The most frequent error is the tendency of nurses to use subjective terms rather than objective information. The use of judgments and opinions is inappropriate because it creates a vague description rather than a clinically precise record, which is so important in proper health care. An example of subjective charting is: "Ate well." Objective reporting would be to say: "Ate all of soft diet except milk."

It is a good idea for nurses to compare their charting techniques with one another to help ensure that proper charting standards are being observed.

What should I chart besides nursing-care interventions and patient observations?

You can never be too detailed when charting. If in doubt whether to chart information, then the information should be charted.

Common items you may overlook include adverse incidents, patient education and counseling, attempts to reach the physician, safety precautions taken and omitted, or incomplete treatments.

Should I chart changes in the patient's condition?

Yes. This is one of the most critical items to chart. Failure to report a change in a patient's condition can readily constitute malpractice because it falls below the accepted standard of care you owe your patient. If the failure to chart a change in condition delays needed treatment, you will be liable for the resultant damages. In many cases, it is equally important for you to chart when *no* change occurs in the patient's condition.

How accurate must charting be concerning the time drugs are administered to a patient?

You should chart the exact time of administration, which is not necessarily the scheduled time. For example, a patient may have a drug scheduled for 8 A.M. but actually receive the drug at 8:45 A.M. This time difference is important because blood levels of particular drugs may be time sensitive. The need for accurate time charting is particularly important with prn ("take as needed") medications.

How often should a patient's condition be charted?

There have been cases where a patient's chart has been without notation for several days. This is poor nursing practice.

The best policy is for you to chart each patient's condition at least once each shift. Even if there has been no significant change in condition, this will show that you paid due attention to the patient.

Is it illegal for me to alter a medical record?

In some states, yes. Several states specify penalties for altering or tampering with medical records. Improper alteration or alteration done for purposes of concealment or with fraudulent intent are criminal or may be in violation of the state's nurse practice act. Generally, the mere correcting of a charting error with no fraudulent intent is permissible.

What should I do if I suspect a patient may sue me and I discover a charting error in that patient's record?

You should never make a correction in this type of situation because the patient or his attorney may already have a copy of the medical record, and an inconsistency will obviously appear suspicious.

The correct approach is not to alter the record but to add the correction to another paper to be attached to the original records.

Can a computer play a role in decreasing recordkeeping errors?

Yes. A well-designed computer system can reduce errors in several important ways.

First, computers reduce the risk of misinterpretation by improving legibility because nurses work from typed orders rather than handwritten ones.

Second, computers reduce misinterpretation by creating standardized formats for assessment reports, flow charts, and care plans. Finally, by time-stamping each entry, computers decrease the chance of scheduling errors.

How can I reduce my legal risks when I am working with computerized medical records?

When you are using a computerized medical record, you have the same liability for errors as when you are working with a manual recordkeeping system.

You can, however, minimize the risk by double checking all patient information entered. Moreover, you should keep private your signature code, to prevent entry by others. Finally, you should indicate whether the physician's orders were written or verbal.

As computerized systems become more common, nurses should be ready to use this technology. It can greatly improve patient care.

Must I verify a physician's order when using computerized records?

Verification is the principal way of reducing error in the computerized record. Checking the accuracy of a doctor's order in a computerized system is the same as signing off on a doctor's order in a manual system. In a computerized system, the unit secretary usually enters a doctor's order into the computer. The order is then held in a "suspense file" until the nurse reviews the entry and checks to be certain the unit secretary interpreted and entered the order correctly. Once the nurse verifies the order, the entry is added to the active record file.

Can computerized records take the place of a manual recordkeeping system?

The JCAH has informally recognized computerized records as legitimate substitutes for manual records. Nevertheless, many states require health facilities with computerized records to maintain a written record system as well.

Computer records can be used under the Federal Controlled Substances Act. There are several technically complex requirements, however, and a hospital should check with the Drug Enforcement Administration before instituting a computerized drug-record system.

Is it dangerous for a physician to leave blank lines between his notes and my notes?

Leaving blank lines between entries on a patient chart can cause legal problems if an entry was inserted out of chronological order or inappropriate information was added to the notes. Either event would create suspicion or be troublesome if the notes were later used in evidence in a malpractice case.

Am I excused from charting a patient's condition and care if the doctor has already written a note adequately covering the patient's condition and care?

No. You are never relieved of your professional responsibilities in charting, even when the doctor's notes adequately document the patient's condition. You must still document your own observations and the nursing care you provided.

What should I do if an adverse incident arises from a nursing error?

You have the duty to file an incident report immediately. You must also report the incident to the physician and institute corrective measures as necessary (before completing the incident report). Any attempt to cover up an error is not only grounds for dismissal but can even increase the potential consequences arising from the error.

Should I write in the medical record that an incident report has been completed?

No. An incident report is not considered clinical information but an administrative tool to reduce future errors.

What is the purpose of an incident report?

The incident report plays two important roles in risk management.

The first is that the report alerts the hospital administrators to the possibility of a patient claim. The hospital (and its insurers) can therefore begin an investigation of the case at the earliest possible time.

Second, the incident report can disclose problem areas and help the administration improve operations in these areas, thereby reducing the likelihood of future problems and claims.

When should an incident report be filed?

An incident report should be filed whenever there is *any* injury to a patient. In addition to patient injuries, medication errors, patient complaints, and injuries to visitors and employees and staff are sufficient reason to file an incident report.

The hospital should precisely define the type of incident subject to report so that every staff member has a clear understanding of when to submit incident reports for events that seem to be outside the hospital's ordinary reporting routine.

Do I have an obligation to complete an incident report when an error in patient care has been made?

Yes, if the error either caused patient injury or may do so in the future. Even if the error may cause insignificant injury, the obligation to report exists.

What information should be disclosed on an incident report?

The incident report should include only the following:

- The name of the patient
- Identification of any witnesses and/or parties to the incident
- A complete narrative of the circumstances and events surrounding the incident
- The observed consequences of the incident to the patient

The format for an incident report should be approved by hospital counsel. Health-care providers, in completing the report, should limit themselves to the specific items contained in the report.

What information should *not* be included in an incident report?

An incident report should not contain the following:

- Opinions, conclusions or assumptions (such as a patient's prognosis)
- Mention of events not observed firsthand by the person completing the report
- Suggestions or opinions of who was responsible for the incident
- Suggestions to prevent the incident from occurring in the future
- Admissions of negligence or liability

This information can, of course, seriously prejudice the defense of any lawsuit arising from the incident.

Should the incident report include statements from other witnesses?

Such items as detailed statements from witnesses, opinions, and other collateral information should not be included in the incident report itself. Instead, this information should be included in a follow-up investigative report conducted by the hospital.

Should an incident report become part of the patient's record?

No. In fact, the patient's record should not even mention the incident report, but should confine itself to clinical information arising from the incident.

Can disclosing the incident in my nursing records take the place of filing an incident report?

No. Entering the incident on your nurse's records does not take the place of completing a separate incident report. Conversely, an incident report does not relieve you of your responsibility to document properly on the patient's chart.

Can a patient's attorney gain access to an incident report?

While courts give parties to a lawsuit wide latitude in discovery (obtaining information from other parties to the lawsuit), the right of a patient or his attorney to an incident report varies from state to state.

To avoid discovery, the hospital or health-care agency may routinely leave the report in possession of its attorney, where it may be held as privileged communication not subject to disclosure. Even with this procedure, there is a reasonable likelihood that a court will order disclosure of the incident report. This should prompt nurses to be extremely careful about how incidents are reported.

Who should complete a patient incident report?

Only a person directly involved in the incident or with firsthand knowledge of the incident should report it. Further, only the person completing the report should sign it. It is usually improper to sign a report describing circumstances or events not personally observed.

If several people observe the incident or have firsthand knowledge, they should each complete a separate incident report. At no time should two or more people join together in submitting one incident report.

How soon after an incident should I complete an incident report?

As soon as possible, preferably on the same day of the incident.

Obviously, with immediate reporting, your recollection of the incident will be clearer. Moreover, the hospital can take corrective action at the earliest possible opportunity, thereby avoiding further liability.

How should an incident report be corrected?

The original incident report should never be erased or crossed out because alterations may be viewed suspiciously, as an attempt to remove an incriminating statement when faced with a malpractice suit. Instead, the incident report should be amended by adding new information or corrected information on a supplemental sheet attached to the original report.

Won't I expose myself to greater risk of liability if I admit to an error in an incident report?

There are very few lawsuits based on an admitted error in a nursing incident report. Obviously, you should carefully consider how the incident is reported; you may even discuss the matter with your supervisor before writing the report. This may help balance your obligation to file the report with the objective of not admitting to liability.

Do RNs and LPNs/LVNs have the same recordkeeping responsibilities?

One of the fundamental legal responsibilities of the nurse is the duty to keep accurate records of the patient's physical and mental condition (e.g., temperature, pulse, and other overt physical signs, as well as emotional behavior). This responsibility is one that is shared by LPNs, LVNs, and RNs alike. Nevertheless, the RN, because of her special training, has the additional responsibility of interpreting and evaluating the patient's symptoms and reactions to any nursing or medical regimen, and to report them to the physician so that he may make appropriate adjustments in the prescribed treatment.

How can I protect myself when I am required to accept a physician's verbal order?

You must be particularly careful to document all the details. This means that the nurse should do the following:

- Record the date and time of the call.
- Review the patient's condition in detail with the physician.
- Record the physician's orders as you listen.
- Read the orders back to the physician.
- Document that the orders were read back to the physician and confirmed.
- Obtain the physician's countersignature as soon as possible.

What information should be contained on a patient's discharge summary?

Although hospital policy should specify what information to include, the discharge summary should at a minimum highlight the patient's condition, his treatment, and his status at discharge. The discharge may also include home-care instruction, the name of the person accompanying the patient, the patient's discharge address, and his mode of transportation from the hospital. A properly completed discharge summary will:

- Summarize patient care.
- Document that the patient has proper information for self-care.
- Provide necessary information for further treatment or readmission.
- Indicate that the hospital complied with the documentation standards of the JCAH.
- Help protect against malpractice claims.

Does the Freedom of Information Act impose any obligation on a hospital to provide a patient access to his records?

Yes. The Freedom of Information Act specifically grants consumers access to their hospital records. Other laws impose an equal duty of disclosure on hospitals. Again, this does not suggest that you must immediately hand over the medical chart to any inquiring patient without following hospital policy.

Who owns a patient's X-rays?

In the absence of any agreement to the contrary, X-rays are universally held to be the property of the physician or the facility that takes the X-ray.

Moreover, it is unclear whether a patient has a legal right to copies of the X-ray, although they can always be subpoened in a judicial proceeding.

It is common practice for patients to transport X-rays from one physician to another when consultation is sought, but the X-ray should ultimately be returned to the physician or facility where it was originally obtained.

Should I accept verbal or telephone orders from a physician?

Not if it can be avoided. Verbal orders are acceptable only in an emergency when the physician cannot immediately attend to the patient. Whenever possible, another nurse should corroborate the order by reading the order back to the doctor. The order should be recorded on the doctor's order sheet as soon thereafter as possible, with the notation "V.O." (for verbal order) or "T.O." (for telephone order). The name of the physician and corroborating nurse should also be recorded, together with the date and time.

You must be certain the physician countersigns the order within the time specified by hospital policy.

Under what circumstances should standing orders be discontinued?

Any significant change in the patient's condition may mean that the standing order is no longer appropriate. Under these circumstances, treatment should be discontinued until the physician can be contacted and authorizes treatment resumed.

9

Confidentiality and Reporting

Questions on the disclosure of medical information are becoming increasingly difficult to answer because of two conflicting trends:

1. The demands for more full reporting by governmental agencies, third-party payers, and others involved in the regulation, financing, or providing of health care
2. State and federal laws aimed at protecting information about private citizens from public disclosure

This chapter continues the discussion begun in the previous chapter by focusing on the legal concepts of privacy and confidentiality, exceptions to these doctrines, and considerations that should go into a decision about releasing confidential information to anyone but the patient.

The chapter also discusses abuse cases because these situations often require reporting and therefore come within the general principles and concerns of this chapter.

Can a physician or a nurse legally disclose a patient's medical condition to inquiring relatives without the patient's consent?

Although physicians and nurses routinely discuss a patient's condition with family members, it is technically improper to do so without the patient's consent.

A patient's consent should be obtained in advance, and when this is impracticable, the discussion should be limited to the most basic facts.

Does the terminally ill patient have a right to demand that no one in his family be told of his diagnosis?

Physicians often do not want to tell dying patients about their condition, but most physicians feel compelled to tell someone. Frequently, the family is informed. When this is done, the patient is deprived not only of his right to know the truth but also of his rights to confidentiality and privacy. It would seem to follow, therefore, that a patient has the right to both make a demand that no one be told and expect his physician to respect it. A civil damage suit for breach of confidentiality would probably be the main legal action a patient could take against a doctor who refused to respect such a demand.

An explicit prohibition by a terminally ill patient on his physician not to tell a family member of his condition implies that the physician has previously discussed the condition with the patient. This is the legally and ethically correct approach.

Can a patient sue for invasion of privacy when his medical information is disclosed to medical or nursing students?

Yes. A patient can successfully sue any unauthorized person who disclosed confidential medical information.

Similarly, a patient can sue for invasion of privacy any unauthorized personnel who observed him without permission.

The only individuals who have a right to observe a patient or have access to medical information are those involved in his medical care. This situation points out the importance of obtaining patient permission for students to participate in a patient's care. It is recommended that this permission be in writing.

Can a patient's problems be discussed at teaching rounds without his permission?

While the technical answer to this question is that unauthorized disclosure is improper, practice in most hospitals is not to tell the patient that his case is being presented.

Doctors in teaching hospitals often tend to believe that when they discuss a case with the house staff or at grand rounds, they are *de facto* helping the patient. Medically, of course, this may be true. Indeed, one of the great advantages of being in a teaching hospital is that the patient is exposed to a great diversity of medical professionals. Such an advantage may, however, be properly considered a major disadvantage by patients who are not told what is occurring and why.

Under the AHA Patient's Bill of Rights, a patient's case may not be presented to "outsiders" in this manner without his express permission. More serious cases occur when the patient is wheeled into a large amphitheater to be put on display before large student audiences. In all cases, the patient has an absolute right to refuse to participate in such teaching activities. When the patient is incapable of granting consent, the hospital should not "volunteer" the patient in this manner.

Are there circumstances when I can legally violate a patient's right to privacy?

Yes. If a patient is exercising the right to privacy in a way that threatens the well-being of others, you may be compelled to violate the patient's confidence. For example, if a patient confides to you that another patient is planning suicide, you would have an obligation to act.

A patient also waivers his right to privacy and confidentiality when he sues you for malpractice. Under these circumstances, it would be unfair to deprive you of the right to disclose information material to your defense.

Don't computerized patient medical records violate the patient's right to privacy?

The most recent U.S. Supreme Court decisions tend to support the right of the hospital to maintain computerized patient records. Nevertheless, the Court noted the potential for abuse inherent in maintaining such records.

Certain safeguards have recently been introduced to protect patient privacy. The major safeguard is the signature code, by which access to the records is limited and controlled.

May a hospital disclose the medical information of a public figure without breaching confidentiality?

A hospital may disclose the patient's general condition. Without the patient's consent, however, the hospital may not disclose the patient's illness, why he is being treated, or the nature of the treatment.

This is particularly true in responding to a reporter or in any case where the information is likely to be disclosed publicly.

May a hospital disclose the identity of patients covered by Medicaid?

No. The patient has the legal right to privacy regarding the source of payment for treatment and care. This right includes access to the highest degree of care without regard to the source of payment for that treatment and care.

Further, the patient has the right, regardless of the source of payment, to examine and receive an itemized and detailed explanation of the total bill for services rendered in the facility.

Is communication between a patient and nurse legally protected so that disclosure cannot be forced?

Only the states of New York, Vermont, Arkansas, and Oregon recognize the nurse–patient relationship as privileged and therefore protected. But other states hold the privilege exists when a nurse follows physician's orders, and the communication between physician and patient is privileged under state law. It is unclear, however, whether the privilege under these circumstances would extend to LPNs/LVNs.

Are there situations where I can be compelled to disclose patient information?

Yes. For example, all states require reporting apparent child-abuse cases. Some states make reporting abuse of the elderly mandatory.

Other states require nurses to disclose information in criminal cases. Further, certain governmental agencies, such as the Internal Revenue Service, Environmental Protection Agency, and Department of Labor, as well as numerous state agencies, have the statutory authority to compel disclosure.

Where the state recognizes communication between patient and nurse as privileged, disclosure can be compelled only when reporting is mandatory by other state laws.

May I safely collect a sample of blood from a person if requested to do so by the police?

If the individual is under arrest, the police can legally order a blood sample to be taken.

If the patient is not under arrest, the forced withdrawal of blood from an individual can pose legal problems. Under these circumstances, you should decline the request unless approved by counsel for the hospital. You must remember that the police can request services from you, but they cannot order you to perform services.

May I report to the police any statements or admissions made by a patient?

That depends on the nature of the statement.

If the patient said, for example, "I burglarized a liquor store," such a statement could be communicated to the police. But if a patient said, "I was shot in the arm when leaving a robbery," that most likely would be a privileged or confidential communication because it relates to the patient's medical condition.

Nurses in every state should review their state's laws to determine whether communication between patients and themselves is in fact privileged or nonprivileged (and therefore subject to disclosure).

What procedures should I follow if I have evidence to be turned over to police?

First, you should carefully document how you came upon the evidence, or performed the clinical procedures if it is clinical evidence. Documentation should include date and time of the collection.

You should then safeguard the evidence until it is turned over to police, to prevent tampering.

You should then record the name of the officer to whom you delivered the evidence, the time and date delivered, and a complete description of the evidence.

Would I have the right to search a patient's belongings for evidence (such as drugs) if requested to do so by police?

Generally, reasonable searches that occur as part of medical practice or hospital policy do not violate a patient's rights. Searches conducted by health practitioners at the request of police, however, would be in violation of the patient's rights unless the police had a valid search warrant.

In all instances, you should refrain from participating

in a search unless it is first approved by the hospital administrator.

May I safely report a case of suspected child abuse without fear of a lawsuit?

The Child Abuse Prevention and Treatment Act, in effect in virtually all states, protects the nurse who, in good faith, reports a case of suspected abuse.

To support a "good faith" filing, you should carefully assess the abused child's condition and other evidence of abuse together with the relationship between the child and the suspected abuser.

To avoid liability, it is important that you avoid direct or personal accusations, or disclosure of your suspicions, to uninvolved third parties.

What is the Child Abuse Prevention and Treatment Act?

In 1973, Congress passed the Child Abuse Prevention and Treatment Act. This federal act requires all states to meet certain uniform standards in order to be eligible for federal assistance in establishing programs to identify, prevent, and treat problems caused by child abuse. This law also established a national center for child abuse and neglect.

As a result of this federal legislation, all states have enacted relatively uniform child-abuse statutes that empower a social welfare or law enforcement bureau to receive and investigate reports of abuse and provide immunity to individuals reporting suspected abuse cases.

Every nurse should be fully knowledgeable about the

child-abuse statute in her state, particularly her responsibility to report child-abuse cases.

How should I respond when faced with an abused-child situation?

There are several guidelines for you to follow:

1. The attending physician should be told of evidence of child abuse so that he may conduct a more thorough body examination.
2. If the child is severely bruised, you should seek an order for a blood coagulation profile.
3. If a parent admits to child abuse and now wants help, the parent should be referred to a local child-abuse center.
4. In all cases, the incident must be reported to the state-designated agency empowered to investigate the decision. You should also notify your supervisor.
5. You should document observations, statements made by the child and/or others, and efforts made to help the child.

Do I have the right to photograph a child whom I suspect has been abused?

If the state law expressly or impliedly permits it, and there is no hospital procedure to prevent it, you can legally photograph the child.

Generally, however, the agency caseworker or the police photograph the child for purposes of obtaining evidence of child abuse. The physician may also photograph the child, unless permission to do so is refused by the parents, in which case the police should immediately be notified.

How should I document a case of suspected child abuse?

You should record the following:

- Any statements or admissions made by the child, the abuser, or other witnesses
- Your own observations
- Your assessment and conclusions, and your reasons for the conclusions
- Steps taken by you to notify child-abuse agencies or others and/or other support provided

What assistance can I provide the police in responding to a child-abuse case?

The most valuable assistance is to advise the police of any danger represented in approaching the suspected abuser.

You should tell the police about the abuser's attitude, whether he or she is under the apparent influence of drugs or alcohol, whether he or she is likely to resist the police physically, and, or course, whether the abuser has any weapons or other means to endanger the police.

This same information should, of course, be provided any child-abuse agency responding to a call for assistance.

Do child-abuse laws also protect abused spouses?

Not ordinarily. Laws protecting abused spouses (or other members of the household) are not as developed as are child-abuse statutes. Nevertheless, many states are now enacting equally protective laws in recognition of the increasing problem of spousal abuse.

Do any states require me to report patient maltreatment in a geriatric facility?

More than half the states have passed elder-abuse laws that make reporting maltreatment of patients a legal responsibility. Several of these states have an ombudsman's office that has the authority to investigate complaints of abuse and the obligation to handle complaints arising from maltreatment in geriatric facilities.

What is the most common complaint of patient abuse in a geriatric facility?

Poor sanitary conditions and inadequate diets are two standard complaints.

The most common medical nursing complaint is the overuse of chemicals (drugs) and physical restraints.

Other common complaints against nurses include the following:

- Failing to make nursing diagnosis
- Delegating improperly
- Failing to document
- Failing to question physician orders
- Failing to insist on proper institutional policies

10

Drugs and Controlled Substances

The use of drugs in medical care is increasing rapidly. Liability claims arising from prescribing, dispensing, and administering drugs is perhaps increasing at an even faster rate because today's medications are particularly toxic and capable of causing great harm.

As a nurse, you not only have the obligation to administer drugs properly from a patient-care viewpoint but, of equal importance, you must also comply with federal and state laws that strictly control the handling of drugs.

Since drug laws are so complex, and various jurisdictions impose specific requirements, every nurse is encouraged to consult local laws and regulations in addition to a review of this chapter.

On what basis would I be held liable when administering medication?

Mistakes in administering medications are among the most common causes of malpractice suits against nurses. Your liability may result from administering the wrong medicine to the wrong patient, in the wrong dose, at the wrong time, or in an improper manner. A frequent cause of medication errors by nurses is misreading a doctor's order or failing to check with the doctor when the order is questionable.

Many medication errors involve faulty technique in giving injections, usually resulting in nerve or tissue injury to the patient. Certainly, not every injury following an injection is attributable to faulty technique on the part of the nurse, but where the onset of injury is immediate and not otherwise explainable, you are generally held liable for negligence in giving the injection.

How should I handle verbal drug orders if I wish to avoid liability?

Verbal medication orders constitute a major source of nursing malpractice cases.

If you receive a verbal drug order, either in person or by telephone, you should do the following:

- Immediately write the order exactly as given.
- Repeat the entire order to the physician.
- Record in ink the drug, dosage, time administered, and such other information as is required by hospital policy.
- Sign or initial the entry.
- Transfer the medication record to the hospital's drug file, if the hospital maintains such a file.

It should be noted that Medicare and JCAH regulations allow use of verbal orders only in emergencies.

Would I be liable if I administered an approved drug for a nonapproved use?

You would not have criminal or administrative liability; however, you might face the risk of increased civil liability.

An unapproved use may include use of the drug for a nonapproved purpose, or through a nonapproved method of administration, or for an excessive and nonapproved dose.

If you are concerned over the safety of such administration, you should decline to administer the drug.

How does the law determine who can legally handle drugs?

In general, most medical nursing and pharmacy practice acts define the specific tasks that belong uniquely to the professional being regulated. Derivatively, unauthorized persons performing the task are unlawfully practicing that particular profession.

In most states, if you as a nurse prescribe a drug, you are practicing medicine without a license. If you go into a pharmacy or drug room and measure out drug dosages, you are unlawfully practicing pharmacy. It is important for nurses to know the limits of their authority when handling drugs.

What is meant by a *legend drug*?

A *legend drug* is any drug marked "Caution—federal law prohibits dispensing without a prescription." That is the "legend" referred to.

The federal Food and Drug Administration determines which drugs are legend drugs, and therefore limited to dispensing on prescription, and which drugs may be safely sold without prescription.

How does a *prescription* differ from a *medication order*?

A *prescription* is an order for medication to be dispensed to or for the patient as ultimate user. A *medication order* is an order for medication intended for immediate administration.

An easier rule is to remember that a prescription is for drugs not intended for institutional administration, whereas a medication order is for an inpatient.

To what extent do states regulate the administration of controlled substances?

Every state has its own controlled substances act, which may be considerably more stringent than the federal controlled substances act.

Therefore, every nurse must understand not only the federal requirements but the state requirements as well. Moreover, a state's nurse practice act may impose even stricter regulations than contained within the state's controlled substances act.

May a physician order "take-home" or discharge medication containing controlled substances via a chart order?

No. Medication orders under Drug Enforcement Administration (DEA) regulations are for medications dispensed for immediate administration, not for a supply of take-home medications, which should be handled by issuance of a prescription.

A medication order for a one- or two-day supply would, however, generally be permissible.

What is meant by a *Schedule* I controlled substance?

Schedule I includes drugs having a high potential for abuse with no currently accepted medical use within the United States. Some of the drugs in Schedule I include heroin, marijuana, LSD, and mescaline.

Because the use of such drugs is stringently limited to research, you as a nurse would not be likely to come in contact with such drugs as part of your routine nursing practice.

Under special permission, a hospital may use Schedule I drugs for research purposes.

What legal steps should I follow before administering a narcotic drug?

You should verify the count in the narcotics drawer and sign the narcotic-control sheet to indicate that the narcotic was administered. If all or part of a narcotic dose is wasted or to be disposed of, then a second nurse should countersign the control sheet.

Are the narcotic recordkeeping requirements governed entirely by the federal Controlled Substances Act?

No. You must also review your state's Controlled Substances Act, nurse practice act, and other applicable state regulations, which may be considerably more stringent than the federal law. Moreover, your hospital's policy may be more strict than applicable law.

What procedures should I follow at the end of my shift concerning narcotics?

You should record the amount of each narcotic on the narcotic checksheet, while the nurse beginning her shift counts the narcotics. If the narcotic checksheet is correct, it should then be signed by you and countersigned by the incoming nurse. If there are any discrepancies, they should be resolved before either nurse leaves the unit.

What is meant by a *proof-of-use sheet*?

Ward stock or a nursing-unit stock of controlled substances is a common procedure in institutional pharmacy practice. The "proof-of-use sheet" is an ancillary disposition record of the drugs for which the record is kept. The patient's chart can also contain the nurse's notation of drugs actually administered, but a proof-of-use record contains the identical information on the ward stock of controlled drugs classified by the name of the drug, rather than the name of the patient.

How should I dispose of excessive amounts of residual and wasted controlled substances?

In a situation typical of hospital medication administration, a physician may order a 50-mg dose of meperidine HCL injection, but only a 75-mg ampule is available. Subject to state law, the federal law permits disposal of the 15-mg excess, provided a written report is made in the hospital narcotic records and provided two nurses witness the disposal and verify by signature or initials the wasted amount, date, and time.

As a nurse practitioner, may I legally prescribe controlled substances?

Yes, in some states. Under federal law, controlled substances may be prescribed by any practitioner authorized to prescribe controlled substances under state law and provided that person either registers with the DEA or is otherwise exempt from registration.

Therefore, you as a nurse practitioner would be authorized to obtain a federal registration from DEA provided you were authorized to do so under state law.

How common is nurse practitioner prescribing in states where it is authorized?

Nurse practitioner (and physician assistant) prescribing is not as prevalent as we would anticipate, primarily because of the greatly increased risks of liability associated with prescribing.

Can I legally dispense drugs?

Unless the state's nurse practice act or pharmacy practice act expressly allows nurse dispensing, you cannot legally dispense drugs. This is within the professional jurisdiction of the pharmacist.

There are instances where nursing supervisors routinely dispense drugs on weekends and evenings when a pharmacist may be unavailable. This does not necessarily make the policy legal.

The hospital (or nursing home) should base policy for dispensing on the authority allowed under state law.

What liability do I have when dispensing drugs from a hospital pharmacy or drug room?

You can be liable for any negligence when you take it upon yourself to dispense drugs from the hospital pharmacy or drug room. In fact, you may be held to the standard of care and level of competence of a registered pharmacist.

Further, if state law does not explicitly allow nurse dispensing, the fact that you violated the law can in itself be used as evidence of negligence, should patient injury result.

Can a physician issue signed blank prescriptions for me to complete at a later date?

No. You have the right to complete a prescription form when specifically authorized to do so by a physician. But you cannot obtain the delegated authority to decide whether a prescription should be issued or when it should be issued. Further, a prescription cannot contain a date beyond the date when it is actually authorized, and postdated prescriptions are illegal.

Can a nursing home patient receive partial orders of Schedule II drugs?

Yes. Although prescriptions for Schedule II drugs must have partial quantities completed within 48 hours, prescriptions for nursing home patients may receive partial quantities with the right to complete the prescription within 6 months from the date of original issue.

Under what circumstances may a long-term-care facility (LTCF) maintain controlled substances in an emergency kit if the facility is not registered by the DEA?

Controlled substances may be placed in an emergency kit in an LTCF that is not registered if the appropriate state agency or regulatory authority specifically approves the placement of such drugs and promulgates procedures to safeguard their control.

Can a foreign-trained physician legally prescribe controlled substances?

A hospital's DEA registration will permit its employed interns, residents, and foreign-trained physicians to prescribe controlled substances for hospital patients provided that the following is true:

1. The prescribing is in the usual course of professional practice.
2. The physician is authorized to do so by the state.
3. The hospital authorizes the physician to prescribe under its DEA registration and assigns a specific internal code number for each physician so authorized.

Nurses should contact the hospital administration if there is any question about any physician's authority to prescribe controlled drugs.

Do I have any special obligations when administering experimental drugs?

Your legal obligations are the same as when dispensing other drugs; however, even more caution is required, considering the particular hazardous nature of the drug.

First, you should carefully review the drug protocol to learn thoroughly about the drug.

Second, you should closely monitor the patient for adverse drug reaction.

Finally, you should be certain that the patient granted informed consent, although obtaining consent is the primary responsibility of the physician.

Under what circumstances may a physician use an investigational-use drug without a patient's informed consent?

Emergency administration is permissible when a patient is in a coma or is otherwise incapable of giving informed consent, his representative cannot be reached, and it is imperative to administer the drug without delay.

What action should I take when a patient is abusing drugs?

You have a duty to act when a patient is abusing either prescription drugs or illicit drugs. If the patient causes injury to himself or others because of drug abuse, you (and the hospital) can be held liable if it can be shown that you had a reasonable basis for being aware of the abuse and did nothing to protect the patient.

Most hospitals have policies for such situations, and these policies should be closely followed. For example, if you are certain the patient is abusing drugs, you ordinarily have the right to conduct a reasonable search for the drug and thereafter confiscate it.

When you merely suspect drug abuse, the right to search depends on whether you had sufficient reason to believe drug abuse was present, and the search was therefore justified. A search may include both the patient's room and personal belongings with these guidelines:

1. Always contact your supervisor before conducting a search or accusing a patient.
2. Tell the patient why you plan to conduct a search and, after the search, notify the patient's physician.
3. Ask a security guard to assist. Besides protecting you, he will serve as a witness to the events.

What procedures should be followed in reporting a colleague for substance abuse?

The best procedure is to convince the colleague to disclose or admit the problem herself. You may also draw on the support of other nurses, or perhaps a trusted clergyman may be able to intervene effectively. The final step would be to inform your immediate supervisor or the hospital administrator, depending on the nature of the problem. Often, the most effective way to change this behavior is to have the employer threaten loss of job unless immediate treatment is obtained.

Policy manuals should contain procedures for reporting problems, and when they exist, they should be followed closely.

Are there any precautions I should take when reporting another nurse for suspected drug theft or other legal violations?

You should discuss the matter only with your immediate supervisor and such other hospital personnel that would have responsibility or authority over the suspected nurse. You should not search a suspected nurse's possessions or private property.

Finally, you should report only observed facts and not make accusations based on assumption.

What precautions should I take when I suspect that a nurse in my department has a substance-abuse or alcohol-addiction problem?

You should report any evidence of another nurse's problem to her immediate nursing supervisor.

The suspected nurse's possessions or private property should not be searched, and no accusations should be made—only report facts. You must be particularly careful to hold the matter confidential from other parties and not spread rumors to injure your colleague's reputation.

Finally, you should refuse to work with a nurse whose professional skills are affected by a drug or alcohol problem because her negligent acts may create liability for those with whom she works.

What safeguards can a hospital take to reduce drug problems among the staff?

A good policy requires the following steps:

- Two nurses must sign for all lost or damaged medications.
- Audits of narcotic administration sheets should be made.
- A medication count should be taken at the beginning and end of each nursing shift.
- Patients should be periodically asked whether they received their medications.
- Frequent observation by a head nurse or supervisor should be made to detect any change in a nurse's behavior.

A hospital can also initiate a support program for addicted personnel.

What responsibility do I have in observing patients taking medication?

The law clearly requires you to observe the patient at reasonable time intervals. Moreover, you are expected to know what a reasonable time interval would be, even if the physician does not order a specific observation period.

How much knowledge am I expected to have about the drugs I administer?

The courts increasingly hold nurses to a higher standard of competency concerning the drugs they administer.

This means that, at a minimum, you are expected to know a drug's safe dosage, limits, toxicity, side effects, indications and contraindications for use, and the proper method and route of administration.

Am I expected to know when a drug is contraindicated in a particular situation?

Yes. There is an increasing trend for nurses to be held liable for drug contraindications. Several court cases have held that the nurse is a medical specialist and that she, along with the physician and pharmacist, has an obligation to know a great deal about the drugs ordered; this knowledge includes drug contraindications.

What should I do if I am uncertain about a particular drug and need more information?

You have an obligation to obtain answers to any drug-related questions you may have before administering the drug. You may readily discover the answers in the *United States Pharmacopeia*, the *Physician's Desk Reference*, *Facts and Comparison*, or other standard drug references.

You may also ask the hospital pharmacist to provide needed drug information. Home-care nurses frequently use the patient's neighborhood pharmacist.

In short, when you are uncertain about a drug, you must ask.

What should I do if I make an error in administering a drug?

You should document the incident thoroughly, as follows:

1. The error should be recorded on the patient's chart together with documentation of the patient's reaction and any medical or nursing interventions taken to prevent or reduce patient harm.
2. You should complete an incident report, fully disclosing the events surrounding the drug error.
3. Most important, you should report the incident to your nursing supervisor and the patient's physician.

Are there any legal advantages to a unit-dose drug distribution system?

Studies disclose a well-designed unit-dose system can substantially reduce the likelihood of error. One reason for this is that tablet or capsule dosage forms are packaged in single-dose blister wrappers with the name and strength of each drug. Therefore, there should be far less error in drug administration.

May I administer injections for new medical conditions without a physician's orders?

No. You may administer injections during a doctor's absence only if the doctor left prn ("as needed") orders. If you administer a drug without orders, you are illegally practicing medicine without a license.

Would nerve injury following injection automatically be proof of injury?

There have been cases in which the fact of nerve injury following an injection has been submitted as proof of negligence, but most courts do not accept this proposition. They require some proof of negligence on the part of the nurse. Most medical practitioners would agree that unforeseen and undesirable reactions from an injection can result from causes other than negligence, including the emotional state and allergenic reaction of the patient, nontraumatic arthritis associated with the injection (but not due to negligence), and the internal condition of the patient before or after an operation. Nurses administering injections are not held liable when the resulting injury is not directly related to improper technique in administering the injection.

You can help protect yourself from charges of negligent administration of injection by recording any relevant information that may give rise to an adverse effect on the patient.

Can a physician lawfully prescribe tranquilizing drugs as a form of restraint?

Tranquilizing or sedative drugs are commonly used to restrain patients. Nevertheless, there is evidence that such drugs are often abused.

The patient's right to the least restrictive treatment means very little if accompanied by the indiscriminate use of drugs as an alternative to physical restraints.

Can I legally change a physician's medication order without his knowledge or consent?

No. To change a prescription is the same as writing a new prescription, which, of course, you cannot legally do.

You can refuse to administer a drug order you believe to be improper, but you have no authority to change it.

Can an LPN or LVN administer drugs?

This depends on the state's nurse practice act.

While a few states still prohibit LPN/LVN drug administration, the majority permit LPNs to give drugs under the supervision of an RN or a physician.

Every LPN must fully understand the limits of her authority for administering drugs.

11

Care of the Dying

In many ways, the increased attention given to the dying is a paradigm for all patients. Dying patients simply present issues more dramatically, since their condition is often the most desperate and stark.

Some of the needs and concerns of dying patients and their caretakers are unique: definition of death, autopsy, organ donation, and orders not to resuscitate. It is also ironic that the most popularly discussed patient right has been the "right to die"; this is the last thing most patients want, and most people would rank access to health care well ahead of cessation of medical intervention. It is well to keep this in mind: Only recently have we allowed an open discussion of death, and we are not yet altogether comfortable with it. Many issues surround the dead and dying about which society has not yet developed a coherent policy.

This chapter focuses on the issues that are most pertinent to the dying patient and on the problems faced by nurses and other professionals charged with care of the dying, including determination of when death has taken place and disposition of the body.

What laws generally cover the "right-to-die" decision?

Virtually every state has either statutes or case-law decisions defining the rights of patients to elect death over artificially or unnecessarily prolonged life. Some states have specific laws relating to death and the care of the dying, such as statutes covering brain death, resuscitation, defibrillation, and drug administration. You should also check your state's nurse practice act because these acts often disclose your responsibility in such situations.

You should also review your hospital's (or nursing home's) policy on this issue. Finally, you should read *The Patient's Right to Choose*: ANA *Viewpoints*.

Do patients have the legal right to choose death?

Yes. The courts have consistently upheld the right of competent adults to decide life-or-death medical choices. With this view, courts have upheld living wills and the ethical view that physicians and nurses may cooperate with patients who want to end their life, although it remains unclear how far health practitioners may go toward that cooperation.

May an incompetent adult refuse life-prolonging treatment, such as chemotherapy or surgery, if death is imminent?

The courts have routinely honored the requests of even the mentally incompetent adult. The court is likely to use the "best interest" test, however, to learn what the patient's views on life support were while he was competent and whether the burden of treatment greatly outweighs the benefits to the patient. The court will also consider the views of the patient's family and physician, and, of course, attempt to assess the degree of patient incompetency and whether the patient understands the consequences of his decision.

Must a hospital allow a patient to refuse treatment, thereby committing euthanasia on hospital premises?

A hospital generally requires a patient to accept basic life support such as food and essential life-sustaining medications while in the hospital. This position is certainly justified in view of the potential civil and even criminal liability arising from such a situation. In several cases, the courts, at the insistence of the hospital, have forced a patient to leave the hospital and return home for purposes of refusing life-sustaining assistance.

Should I attempt resuscitation on a terminally ill patient who rejects treatment?

Although this issue remains a most complex and controversial issue for modern nursing, the safest practice is to call a code. Of course, the preferable alternative would be to get the doctor to issue a no-code order before the medical crisis occurs. No-code/slow-code orders are fraught with legal consequences when there is an unsigned verbal no-code.

Must I follow a verbal order not to resuscitate?

No. Good medical practice requires that all physician's orders be documented and written on the physician's order sheet, and often in the patient's progress notes as well. This practice can be compromised only in emergency situations. Since there is almost by definition no such thing as an emergency order not to resuscitate, verbal orders not to resuscitate are improper and should not be followed by anyone.

It is accepted medical practice to document all such orders carefully in both the patient's progress notes and in the physician's order sheet, to have the physician sign the order, and to have the order include an explanation of why it is given.

What is meant by a *slow-code order*?

Any unwritten or undocumented no-code order is a so-called *slow-code order*.

Slow-code orders are considered illegal in every state and should not be honored. Only written no-code orders offer legal validity and protection.

How does a slow-code order differ from a *limited code*?

A limited code limits the measures to be taken to resuscitate a patient. A limited code is lawful.

What should I do if a physician gives a verbal slow-code order, but refuses to countersign the documentation of the order?

You should insist on countersigning by the physician. If the physician refuses, you should document the refusal and bring the matter to the attention of your supervisor. Most hospitals have specific procedures to follow in this instance; if your hospital does not, it should establish a policy. In the final analysis, if the physician continues to refuse documentation, you should disregard the slow-code order and attempt resuscitation.

Are slow-code orders legal?

No. If you carry out a slow-code order and fail to resuscitate the patient, you can be liable for the wrongful death of the patient.

Slow-codes should never be agreed to or undertaken by members of a health-care team. Either lifesaving treatments should be administered properly, or lifesaving treatments are to be legally withheld.

How can I avoid a slow-code order?

You must insist that every no-coded patient have a written order. Unless the physician has written a no-code order or has signed his verbal order, you should always initiate resuscitation efforts in a patient in cardiac or respiratory arrest.

You must remember that if a lawsuit results from involvement in a patient's death because of slow-coding, you will have no written evidence that the doctor gave a verbal no-code order.

One way for you to provide evidence that a physician gave a verbal, unsigned no-code order is to keep a personal journal to document slow-codes that occur on the unit. This journal should be written in ink, dated, and signed by you after each entry.

Are no-code orders legal?

When a patient is terminally ill and imminent death is expected, it is common for the patient's family (and physician) to agree that a no-code order is appropriate.

The correct procedure is for the physician to write the

order and for the staff to follow it, and then to refuse treatment when the patient goes into cardiac or respiratory arrest.

This is considered a legal order. You will incur no liability under this procedure, providing the order was written by the physician.

If a terminally ill patient expressly states that he does not want to be coded, can I honor this request in the absence of a physician's no-code order?

If a terminally ill patient has indicated he does not want treatment, you would be violating his rights to refuse treatment if you attempted resuscitation. Yet, if you refuse treatment, you are practicing medicine without a license and can incur both criminal and civil liability.

In a double-bind situation such as this, you should document the patient's statement and chart the patient's condition and apparent mental competence at the time. The patient's physician should be told of the patient's wishes as soon as possible so that he can decide whether to issue a no-code order.

What if the physician issues a no-code order for a patient whose death does not appear imminent?

If you dispute the appropriateness of a physician's no-code order, you have both a legal and a professional responsibility to question the order. This is consistent with your independent responsibility to use professional judgment in caring for the patient.

In this situation, you can delay or refuse to carry out

the order until the physician either corrects, confirms, or rescinds the order to your satisfaction.

Before approaching the physician, you should document your assessment of the patient's condition. If the physician refuses to change the order or is unable to convince you of its appropriateness, you should bring the matter to the attention of your supervisor. In all events, you should refuse to follow the order if questions as to its validity remain.

Can a patient's family issue a no-code order, or must it come from the physician?

You cannot accept a no-code order from a patient's spouse or other relative. Only the physician can issue such an order. Of course, the physician should be made aware of the family's preference, and often the desires of the family encourage the no-code order.

What should I do if I question the legality of an order to discontinue life-support efforts?

Because the law on this issue is complex, you should always seek an opinion from the hospital's legal department if a question of legality arises.

You should also insist that the order be in writing and that the medical record discloses a justification for the action.

Finally, you must be particularly careful in documentation and supply a complete record of continuing care, indicating precisely how and when each treatment was terminated.

Can I refuse to obey a no-code order if it violates my religious beliefs?

Yes. But if the no-code order is valid, you cannot impose your religious beliefs on the patient.

In this instance, you should request substitute duty. This is also recommended when you have an exceptionally close attachment to the patient and may encounter emotional problems in fulfilling the no-code order.

Can a relative override a patient's wishes about donation of body organs after the patient dies?

Not if the patient has properly complied with the provisions of the Uniform Anatomical Gift Act of the state in which he is a resident. The gift legally takes effect immediately on death and is therefore binding on relatives. As a matter of policy, however, few hospitals will follow the deceased's wishes over strong family objections.

Does organ donation affect funeral and burial arrangements?

No. The removal of organs does not interfere with customary funeral or burial arrangements. These remain the responsibility of the family, except when a body is donated for medical training, in which case the donee institution accepts responsibility for proper burial.

Does hospice care change the risks in attending to the terminally ill patient?

Hospice care shifts the emphasis of care from the customary goal of preserving life to what is often the more realistic goal: providing quality care for the remaining life of the terminally ill patient.

By focusing on alleviating pain and suffering and by providing psychosocial and emotional support, as well as medical support, health-care professionals give the patient an increased chance for a natural, humane, dignified, ethical, and less legally complicated approach to death.

Hospice care resolves the many legal complications related to such issues as informed consent, "no-code" orders, and liability for involvement in euthanasia. Hospice care has been routinely accepted by the courts as an accepted way to approach death with dignity.

Do dying patients have the right to narcotic drugs for pain relief?

The general answer is that while there is no specific legal right, as a matter of public policy, narcotic and other pain-relieving drugs should be made freely available to dying patients. Experience demonstrates that to be therapeutically effective, doses need not be so high as to distort reality. Also, arguments that these drugs should be denied terminally ill patients because they might become addicted or chromosomes might be damaged are, of course, foolish under the circumstances.

In places in which drugs have been used, much success has been reported in alleviating patient suffering while helping patients learn to accept death as a natural event.

What is the ANA's position on "right-to-die" issues?

The ANA has emphasized the right of competent patients to participate in making decisions about their health and in evaluating the health care they receive. The ANA has supported this right in two documents, the ANA Code for Nurses and its Social Policy Statement.

The ANA Code says that each patient, including the terminally ill or dying patient, has these rights:

- To decide what treatment he will accept or reject
- To receive the information needed to make informed decisions
- To be warned of possible side effects of different treatments

The Social Policy Statement says that nurses must respect each patient's right to self-determination and independence and that nurses must recognize their patient's dignity.

Implicit in these rights is the "right to die," a position not always sanctioned by the various states.

How can I help family members cope with the loss of a loved one?

You must often go beyond the clinical role and become supportive to family members when death occurs. This is particularly so when you have established a close relationship with family members in the course of patient care.

A family may welcome your support in a time of crisis. Often, you can encourage family members to express their feelings and help them cope by encouraging them to use supportive services, such as the hospital's chaplain.

In short, you must be a nurse in the fullest sense of the word: a professional who is both caring and compassionate.

What should I do if my patient makes a dying declaration?

A dying declaration is a statement made in anticipation of death. It is generally admissible in court as evidence on the premise that such statements are usually truthful.

When you receive an oral statement, you should document what is being said as close to word-for-word as possible. You should also document the name of other witnesses to the declaration and the patient's condition at the time. Whenever possible, you should also enlist the aid of other witnesses, who can corroborate the verbal declaration.

Once recorded or reduced to written form, the written statement should be delivered to the patient's physician and your nursing supervisor. This keeps them informed and alerts them that an item in the patient's medical records may have legal significance.

What procedures should I follow when I am asked to witness a will?

In all states, a nurse's signature on a will simply signifies that she saw the patient sign the will and that she also observed the other witnesses sign. Some states require the testator to declare the document to be his or her last will and testament in the presence of the witnesses.

You should refrain from providing legal advice, preparing the will, or influencing the patient's decisions relative to the will.

Should I record my role when acting as a witness to a patient's will or legal document?

It is sound practice for you to record in your notes whenever you act as a witness for a patient. Your notes should also reflect the patient's observed condition, other parties present, and other events relating to the signing. Many hospitals also require that they be notified when hospital personnel serve as witnesses to a will or other legal document.

What is the legal significance of my signing a document as a witness?

When you sign as a witness, you certify only that you saw a person known to you by name execute the document. Being a witness does not necessarily signify that the patient had competency to sign or that the signature was not of the patient's own free will. Of course, you should never witness a document if you believe the patient to be incompetent or subject to fraud or duress.

Can I incur liability when I act as a witness?

Yes. You can be liable if it can be shown that you violated the prevailing standard of care when acting as a witness. This would include situations where a signature was false or the patient was clearly incompetent. You can also be liable if you knowingly allow a minor, nonguardian, or other ineligible person to sign a document for which he or she lacks capacity or authority.

What is meant by a *living will*?

In a living will, a person declares the medical procedures he wants and does not want performed when he is terminally ill. Generally, the will applies only to comatose patients who can no longer communicate their wishes to terminate life-support systems.

The will is called a *living* will because, unlike testamentary wills, it takes effect before death.

A living will is often called a "right-to-die" or "death with dignity" form.

Are living wills valid and enforceable?

Every state recognizes the validity of a living will as a legal document. This does not mean that a living will is necessarily binding or enforceable.

Currently, only 22 states and the District of Columbia recognize living wills as legally binding. Of these states, some impose penalties for noncompliance, while others impose no penalties for noncompliance, making living wills advisory only.

Who can make a living will on behalf of a mentally incompetent adult?

Only Arkansas allows a competent adult to make a living will on behalf of an adult who is mentally incompetent. In all other states, only the concerned individual can make a living will; presumably, an incompetent adult does not have the legal capacity to make a valid living will.

Can minors make a living will?

Although minors cannot make a valid testamentary will, at least three states—Arkansas, Louisiana and New Mexico—allow parents to make living wills for their children.

Of course, a parent can always decide that extraordinary medical procedures not be used to prolong a child's life, nullifying the need for a living will. Conversely, if the child wants to die but the parents insist on prolonged efforts, the wishes of the parents will prevail.

Can a patient's family override a living will and order continuation of life-support procedures against a patient's wishes?

No. In fact, many states make it illegal deliberately to destroy or conceal the existence of a living will.

In a state that does not recognize a living will, the health-care team should carefully balance the wishes of the patient against the wishes of the family.

Can I legally administer drugs (i.e., an overdose of morphine) to facilitate death to a terminally ill patient who executed a living will?

No. Even if death appears imminent, you cannot take overt steps to facilitate death. This must be distinguished from a no-code procedure where the medical staff can legally withhold extraordinary efforts to prolong life.

If you actively participate in accelerating death—even with a physician's orders—you can be guilty of manslaughter or even murder. Such actions on your part could impose considerable civil liability as well.

Can a living will be verbal?

No. Every state requires a written document. Should a patient verbally make his wishes known, however, you should immediately and completely record the patient's statement in his medical records. Once aware of his wishes, most families and physicians will comply with the patient's request.

How are living wills prepared?

Typical state laws require that a living will be written, signed, and witnessed. While the patient's attorney may prepare the living will, forms are also available from numerous state agencies and from the Society for the Right to Die, 250 West 57 Street, New York, NY 10107.

Should I be a witness to a patient's living will?

Many states do not allow nurses or other health-care providers to be witnesses to their patients' living wills. Even when it is not prohibited, it is usually unwise for nurses to witness the living will of patients for whom the nurse has a professional responsibility.

How can a patient revoke a living will?

There are a number of ways to revoke a living will. The patient may simply tear it up or mark it *revoked* or *canceled*. The patient may also request medical care inconsistent with the living will. A court may also invalidate a living will made years earlier when the patient's circumstances may have been different. This underlines the need for the patient periodically to update any living will as an expression of current intent.

Some states, for example Wisconsin, automatically revoke a living will after a defined number of years.

Is the living will from another state valid if the patient moves to a new state?

If the new state recognizes living wills, it will generally honor the living will prepared in another state. If the new state does not require recognition of a living will, it may or may not choose to recognize the patient's living will.

Can a foreign citizen make a living will that will be held valid in the United States?

Yes. A foreign citizen may prepare a living will, and it will be honored to the same extent as a living will prepared by a U.S. citizen. If the individual prepared a living will in a foreign country, it will be recognized to the same extent a living will prepared in another state would be recognized.

Where should a patient retain copies of his living will?

Properly signed and witnessed living wills should be left with the patient's family and his physician, and with his medical records in the hospital, to ensure availability at the appropriate time.

Can a living will be prepared in advance of a terminal illness?

Most states allow a living will to be prepared in advance of a diagnosis of terminal illness. California and Texas require that it be prepared after such a diagnosis.

Are living wills recognized in Canada?

No Canadian province has yet approved of living wills. And the Canadian Law Reform Commission has rejected the concept of living wills.

What should I do if I find a living will attached to a patient's chart or medical records?

You should first notify your supervisor and the patient's physician.

The next step should be to obtain the hospital's policy as to honoring living wills. The hospital administrator, the patient's physician, or both should then call the living will to the attention of the patient's family.

Finally, and most important, if the patient remains capable of communication, he should be asked about the living will and whether he wants it to remain in effect. The family member or health-care provider who may enjoy the closest rapport with the patient should be chosen for this task.

What should I do if the concept of a living will is contrary to my religious beliefs?

The only proper alternative is for you to call the situation to the attention of your supervisor and request reassignment where you will no longer be responsible for caring for this patient.

Are living wills binding on physicians?

Although many states accept the validity of living wills, only Kansas, California, Texas, and the District of Columbia impose penalties on physicians who refuse to comply with a patient's request.

Are doctors and nurses immune from criminal and civil liability in carrying out actions consistent with a patient's living will?

If doctors, nurses, and other health-care providers follow the wishes expressed in a living will, they are generally immune from civil and criminal liability. In states without living wills, however, absolute immunity cannot be assured.

Because the legal consequences of complying with living wills can be uncertain and can vary from state to state, nurses and other health-care providers should confer with their employer before adopting a personal policy on this issue.

May I be a witness to a living will or a "death with dignity" request?

Many states provide that the nurse cannot legally witness such a document on behalf of the patient because of an obvious conflict of interest. Several states allow nurses to witness living wills for patients not under their direct care.

What is a *durable power of attorney*, and how does it differ from a living will?

A durable power of attorney permits the patient to appoint an individual authorized to make medical decisions on his behalf should he become comatose or unable to act for himself. Usually a durable power of attorney becomes effective only on the incapacity of the grantor.

Most states recognize the validity of a durable power of attorney. It remains unclear, however, whether the person authorized to act has the express or implied authority to terminate life-support efforts. Therefore, a patient may want to use both a power of attorney and a living will.

Can life-support treatment be withheld from a minor who is terminally ill and has expressed a desire to die?

No. If a patient is a minor or has never been competent, life-support treatment cannot be withheld without a court order. And except in states with natural-death acts, a court order is necessary to withdraw treatment once it has been initiated.

How is death legally determined?

Many state legislatures have passed laws that define *brain death*, now the prevailing procedure for determining death. Other states accept brain death as the determinant by case-law decisions.

Still, a number of states do not officially recognize brain death and force the physician to rely on classical clinical characteristics, such as a flat ECG or EKG, absence of respiration, and failure to respond to stimuli.

Have there been any efforts to adopt a universal definition of death?

In 1980, the American Bar Association, the American Medical Association, and the Uniform Law Commission drafted the Uniform Determination of Death Act. Under their definition, "a patient who has suffered either irreversible cessation of circulatory and respiratory function or irreversible cessation of all functions of the entire brain stem, is dead."

These medical standards are observed in many states, but no state has formally adopted this definition.

Why is brain death increasingly used in the determination of death?

One reason is that the (earlier) pronouncement of death resulting from the brain-death standard increases the chances of a successful organ transplant when the patient is a donor. Because medical equipment can often maintain respiration and circulation, some patients artificially "live" after their brain becomes irreversibly dead.

Can I legally pronounce death?

No. All states currently reserve this right to physicians. If a physician cannot personally observe the patient, however, the physician can pronounce death on receipt of information telephoned by the nurse.

In such situations, the nurse should accurately chart the details of the communication.

You are usually not held liable for a wrongful determination of death because this is the responsibility of a physician, even when the conclusion is reached on physical or clinical symptoms communicated by you.

Some states are planning enactment of laws permitting nurses to determine death when such death was expected and/or occurred in a nursing home or in the home of the patient.

May I notify the family of a patient's death?

This is almost always undertaken by the physician or hospital administrator, and it is not considered a proper function of the nurse.

In many situations, a physician is not present, and the nurse does communicate with the family while waiting for the physician. These instances should be handled as tactfully as possible, avoiding any conclusive pronouncement of death.

What legal responsibility may I have in preparing a dead body for removal to the morgue?

Your primary responsibility is to make certain the patient is identified properly and there is no misidentification. In several cases, nurses have been held liable for causing a mixup in the identification of deceased patients.

Who has the responsibility for the burial of a deceased patient?

The family member who has the right to consent to autopsy has the reciprocal obligation to bury the body. Some courts have held this to be the responsibility of the executor or administrator of the estate, however.

When a family member cannot be located or refuses to bear burial responsibility, the state or county must dispose of the body. This is generally accomplished by donating the body to a medical school or other recognized research institution.

What is a *legal* or *official* autopsy?

This is an autopsy performed to determine the cause of death when foul play may have contributed to the death. The circumstances under which such autopsies are performed are set out by the state medical examiner's or the coroner's statutes. If the state official responsible for performing such autopsies deems one necessary (e.g., suspected homicide, suicide, violent death, or accidental death), no permission of the family is necessary, nor can the family prevent the autopsy from being performed.

Who can grant consent for an autopsy?

This is usually defined by state law. Many laws simply list the relatives authorized to give consent. Others specify which relatives can grant consent in descending order of authority. The most common order is spouse, adult children, parents, brothers and sisters, and grandparents.

If the death came under the jurisdiction of a medical examiner or coroner, the decision to perform an autopsy rests solely with him, whether the family grants consent or not.

Why would a patient's family want an autopsy performed?

If the cause of death is potentially genetic and treatable, or if it is infectious, the exact determination of cause of death may be helpful to other family members. Also, if the cause of death may have been related to medical malpractice, autopsy findings may help prove this. The deceased or his family may also wish to make a contribution to medical education or research, and therefore want to know the precise cause of death.

Who is responsible for paying the cost of an autopsy?

If a hospital physician requests the autopsy from the family, the cost of the autopsy is almost universally absorbed by the hospital and does not appear as a separate item on the patient's bill.

When the autopsy is solely at the family's request, however, the cost is borne by the patient's estate.

Of course, autopsies ordered by a coroner or medical examiner are undertaken at government expense.

For what purpose would a hospital want to perform an autopsy on a deceased patient?

Teaching hospitals view the percentage of autopsies performed as a measure of the adequacy of their teaching program. Autopsies can confirm the suspected cause of death, help train doctors, and be useful in research projects. To be approved for internships and residencies by the AMA's Council on Medical Education, a hospital must provide proper facilities for postmortem examinations and maintain a high percentage of autopsies. A hospital may not be approved that does not maintain an autopsy rate of at least 25% of its deaths, exclusive of stillbirths and autopsies ordered by legal authorities.

Can the hospital retain any portion of the body after autopsy?

No. The hospital cannot retain any tissues or organs without the permission of the person who consented to the autopsy. Standard forms for permission generally include permission to retain samples, and the rule against retention does not cover limited small portions of organs taken for further study. The person consenting to the autopsy, however, has the right to place whatever limitations on the consent he wishes.

12

Ethical Issues

Abortion, contraception, sterilization, and organ transplants are but a few of the far-reaching and dramatic ethical issues that show how changes in the law can affect medical practice and the rights of both patients and their providers.

Laws on many of these issues are both obscure and controversial because their resolution necessarily cuts across a broad spectrum of medical, legal, religious, and personal considerations. Yet nurses have responsibilities within these areas.

This chapter highlights the most commonly encountered situations where nursing intervention is likely.

What is the current law on abortions?

The Supreme Court ruling in *Roe* v. *Wade* (1973) protects a woman's right to privacy in having an abortion during the first trimester of pregnancy. After the first trimester, a state may regulate the conditions of abortion. In the third trimester, abortions are allowed only when necessary to protect the mother's health.

Can a state impose any regulations on how abortions shall be performed during the first trimester of pregnancy?

While the Supreme Court upheld viability as the earliest point at which a state can interfere with or regulate a woman's right to have an abortion, it appears that a state has some regulatory rights even during the first trimester. These regulatory rights include requirements that a licensed physician perform the abortion and that adequate records be maintained. Conversely, a state cannot require the abortion to be performed in a hospital accredited by the JCAH.

Does a minor require parental consent to have an abortion?

No. Recent U.S. Supreme Court decisions make clear that a state cannot stop a mature or otherwise emancipated minor from obtaining an abortion without parental consent.

If there is a question as to the competency of a minor to make her own decision, a judge may be required to certify that the minor is sufficiently mature to grant consent.

Some states do require a hospital to notify parents when performing an abortion on a minor.

Can a secular hospital refuse to perform abortions for secular reasons?

Recent Supreme Court decisions suggest a hospital cannot invoke its own religious or secular doctrines as a reason for refusing abortions.

Can I legally refuse to assist in the performance of an abortion if it is against my religious convictions?

Some states have laws granting nurses a "conscience" right to refuse to participate in abortions for religious or moral reasons.

Although hospitals in other states can legally require nurses to participate in abortions against their consent, as a practical matter very few do.

If you have conflicts about abortion, they should be discussed before you accept employment. In no event should the conflict be discussed with the patient.

Where can I locate organizations that advocate for legislative action in relation to abortion?

Two prominent organizations include the National Right to Life Committee (NRLC) and the National Abortion Rights Committee (NARAC).

The NRLC focuses closely on fetal rights and is an advocate of fetal rights at time of conception. Conversely, NARAC recognizes maternal rights but favors abortion as an alternative to unwanted pregnancies.

Do minors have less right to contraceptives (or contraception advice) than they do to abortions?

No. A 1977 U.S. Supreme Court decision ruled unconstitutional various state laws that are more stringent as to contraception than to abortion. Therefore, laws about contraception can be equally rigid or less rigid than laws dealing with abortion, but they cannot be more rigid.

Based on this decision, a minor would have the right

to contraceptives and contraception advice without parental consent and often without parental notification.

Under what circumstances must a hospital provide sterilization services?

A government hospital, or one sufficiently involved in government activities, cannot permit certain surgical procedures and, at the same time, ban others involving reproduction that involve no greater risk or demand on staff and facilities. A municipal hospital's ban on the performance of sterilizations, for example, has been found to be illegal as a violation of the equal protection clause of the Fourteenth Amendment to the Constitution. In like manner, these hospitals cannot prevent qualified staff physicians from performing abortions in the hospital.

A hospital would, however, have the right to refuse such services, not as a matter of policy, but when it in good faith cannot adequately or properly perform the requested service.

Is the informed consent of the research subject always necessary for lawful experimentation involving human subjects?

Yes. Informed consent is a necessary precondition to lawful human experimentation, but informed consent is not alone a sufficient precondition. Other requirements, such as the reasonableness of the experiment and review and approval by an institutional review board or appropriate institutional committee, are necessary to prevent patient abuse or unjustified medical procedures that appear only as needless experimentation.

Can parents give legal authorization for medical experiments to be performed on their children?

There are a number of ways of classifying experiments. For our purposes the most useful are the following:

1. An experimental treatment or procedure aimed at curing the child's condition
2. An experimental procedure aimed at finding out more about the child's condition
3. An experimental procedure designed to learn more about the disease from which the child is suffering
4. An experimental procedure designed to learn something that might benefit others but will not benefit the child

The first two types of experiments can be consented to by parents. Under proper conditions, the third might also be consented to, if, for example, there is no known cure or treatment for a disease and experimenting on children suffering from it is the only way to develop one. It is within the fourth area that decisions are the most difficult. It is arguable, for example, that parents have no legal right to subject their children to experiments that cannot be of reasonable benefit to the children. In support, the U.S. Supreme Court has repeatedly said that while parents are free themselves to become martyrs, they are not free to make martyrs of their children.

Still other cases conclude that even with the consent of the child and parents, a court of law must necessarily sanction the experiment. This, for example, has been the major thrust of cases dealing with kidney transplants involving minors. One court has gone so far as to say that no one, not even the court, can authorize the taking of a kidney from a child. The better view would appear to be that the only instance in which experimentation on children should be permitted is under the supervision of a court with a court-appointed guardian. The duty of the guardian would be impartially to represent the interests of the children in the experiment, to ascertain that there was sufficient benefit to the child to justify a procedure that might otherwise be viewed as experimental.

Can a mentally ill patient be used in medical research?

This issue raises many unresolved questions. The prevailing rule is that both voluntary and involuntary residents of an institution have the constitutional right to be protected from harm. The proper authority—typically a research proposal review board—should allow the patient to participate in research only if it is appropriate to his needs or the needs of others with his type of mental disorder.

How does an individual consent to an organ transplant?

The Uniform Anatomical Gift Act, adopted in all 50 states, provides that any competent adult can donate specified organs (or the entire cadaver) by completing and signing a uniform-donor card in the presence of two witnesses. In many states, this intent is recorded on the reverse side of a driver's license. These forms are usually available from the Red Cross, major hospitals, and various state agencies and charitable organizations.

Who is responsible for determining when death occurs for purposes of organ transplant?

The physician in attendance is responsible for determining the precise moment of death. Most state donation statutes specify, however, that the doctor attending the dying person not participate in either the removal or the transplantation but that the transplant procedure be left to other physicians.

May a minor refuse to participate as an organ transplant donor against the wishes of his parents?

At least one case supports the view that a minor may refuse to be an organ donor—even against the wishes of his parents. For example, a twin may refuse to donate a kidney to his twin, as the courts uphold the rights of a minor to consent to surgical procedures and grant to minors the same rights of privacy as an adult enjoys.

Who may authorize donation of a decedent's organs?

A family member may authorize donation by signing an appropriate donation document. If death occurs within 24 hours of admission to a hospital, however, or results from an accident, homicide, or other unnatural cause, a medical examiner will also be required to grant consent.

What responsibility do I have in connection with a prospective organ donor?

You have no mandated responsibility in obtaining proper consent because this is a medical responsibility.

You can, however, play a decisive role in familiarizing patients with the organ-donor process and, of course, act as an important source of objective information.

If you have reason to be opposed to the procedure for a particular patient, you should share your concerns with the appropriate medical staff, the hospital administrator, or both.

What are the age requirements for an individual to become an organ donor?

Both in the United States and Canada, any person 18 years or older may choose to become an organ donor.

Who can consent to an organ transplant for a minor or for a mentally incompetent adult?

Generally, a parent or legal guardian has the same valid authority to consent to an organ transplant as for any other medical or surgical procedure.

Some states, however, allow an organ transplant only if the donor is a minor or if the donor and the recipient are related.

Can the family of a deceased person rescind the person's desire to be an organ donor?

Technically, the decision of an individual to donate an organ is legally binding on his family.

In practical terms, few hospitals go against the wishes of family members if they choose not to proceed with the donation.

Considering the shortage of organs for transplant and other life-sustaining resources, how do medical ethics boards decide who lives and who dies?

This is undoubtedly one of the most sensitive issues in modern health care.

Before allowing for extraordinary measures, such as transplants, medical ethics boards will consider whether the patient will be able to cope with the results and the extent to which the transplant will either extend life or improve the quality of life.

APPENDICES

A

NLN *Patient's Bill of Rights*

The National League for Nursing believes nurses are responsible for upholding these rights of patients:

- People have the right to health care that is accessible and that meets professional standards, regardless of the setting.
- Patients have the right to courteous and individualized health care that is equitable, humane, and given without discrimination as to race, color, creed, sex, national origin, source of payment, or ethical or political beliefs.
- Patients have the right to information about their diagnosis, prognosis, and treatment—including alternatives to care and risks involved—in terms they and their families can readily understand, so that they can give their informed consent.
- Patients have the legal right to informed participation in all decisions concerning their health care.
- Patients have the right to information about the qualifications, names, and titles of personnel responsible for providing their health care.
- Patients have the right to refuse observation by those not directly involved in their care.
- Patients have the right to privacy during interview, examination, and treatment.

- Patients have the right to privacy in communicating and visiting with persons of their choice.
- Patients have the right to refuse treatments, medications, or participation in research and experimentation, without punitive action being taken against them.
- Patients have the right to coordination and continuity of health care.
- Patients have the right to appropriate instruction or education from health-care personnel so that they can achieve an optimal level of wellness and an understanding of their basic health needs.
- Patients have the right to confidentiality of all records (except as otherwise provided for by law or third-party payer contracts) and all communications, written or oral, between patients and health-care providers.
- Patients have the right of access to all health records pertaining to them, the right to challenge and to have their records corrected for accuracy, and the right to transfer of all such records in the case of continuing care.
- Patients have the right to information on the charges for services, including the right to challenge these.
- Above all, patients have the right to be fully informed as to all their rights in all health-care settings.

The National League for Nursing urges its membership, through action and example, to demonstrate that the profession of nursing is committed to the concepts of patients' rights.

B

AHA *Patient's* Bill *of* Rights

Most hospitals design their own patient's bills of rights. The American Hospital Association's bill of rights, shown below, is one of the bills they use as a model.

A *Patient's* Bill *of* Rights

1. The patient has the right to considerate and respectful care.

2. The patient has the right to obtain from his physician complete current information about his diagnosis, treatment, and prognosis in terms the patient can be reasonably expected to understand. When it is not medically advisable to give such information to the patient, it should be made available to an appropriate person in his behalf. He has the right to know, by name, the physician responsible for coordinating his care.

3. The patient has the right to receive from his physician information necessary to give informed consent prior to the start of any procedure and/or treatment. Except in emergencies, such information for informed consent should include but not necessarily be limited to the specific procedure and/or treatment, the medically significant risks involved, and the probable duration of incapacitation. Where medically significant alternatives for care or treatment exist, or when the patient requests information concerning medical alternatives, the patient has the right to such information. The patient has the right to know the name of the person responsible for the procedures and/or treatment.

4. The patient has the right to refuse treatment to the extent permitted by law and to be informed of the medical consequences of his action.

5. The patient has the right to every consideration of his privacy concerning his own medical care program. Case discussion, consultation, examination, and treatment are confidential and should be conducted discreetly. Those not directly involved in his care must have the permission of the patient to be present.

6. The patient has the right to expect that all communications and records pertaining to his care should be treated as confidential.

7. The patient has the right to expect that within its capacity a hospital must make reasonable response to the request of a patient for services. The hospital must provide evaluation, service, and/or referral as indicated by the urgency of the case. When medically permissible, a patient may be transferred to another facility only after he has received complete information and explanation concerning the needs for and alternatives to such a transfer. The institution to which the patient is to be transferred must first have accepted the patient for transfer.

8. The patient has the right to obtain information as to any relationship of his hospital to other health-care and educational institutions insofar as his care is concerned. The patient has the right to obtain information as to the existence of any professional relationships among individuals, by name, who are treating him.

9. The patient has the right to be advised if the hospital proposes to engage in or perform human experimentation affecting his care or treatment. The patient has the right to refuse to participate in such research projects.

10. The patient has the right to expect reasonable continuity of care. He has the right to know in advance what appointment times and physicians are available and where. The patient has the right to expect that the hospital will provide a mechanism whereby he is informed by his physician or a delegate of the physician of the patient's continuing health-care requirements following discharge.

11. The patient has the right to examine and receive an explanation of his bill, regardless of source of payment.

12. The patient has the right to know what hospital rules and regulations apply to his conduct as a patient.

C

ACLU *Patient's Bill of Rights*

The American Civil Liberties Union has developed this patient's bill of rights as a model for any health institution wishing to develop its own.

Preamble: As you enter this health-care facility, it is our duty to remind you that your health care is a cooperative effort between you as a patient and the doctors and hospital staff. During your stay a patient's rights advocate will be available to you. The duty of the advocate is to assist you in all the decisions you must make and in all situations in which your health and welfare are at stake. The advocate's first responsibility is to help you understand the role of all who will be working with you, and to help you understand what your rights as a patient are. Your advocate can be reached at any time of the day by dialing______. The following is a list of your rights as a patient. Your advocate's duty is to see to it that you are afforded these rights. You should call your advocate whenever you have any questions or concerns about any of these rights.

- The patient has a legal right to informed participation in all decisions involving his/her health-care program.
- We recognize the right of all potential patients to know what research and experimental protocols are being used in our facility and what alternatives are available in the community.
- The patient has a legal right to privacy regarding the source of payment for treatment and care. This right includes ac-

cess to the highest degree of care without regard to the source of payment for that treatment and care.

- We recognize the right of a potential patient to complete and accurate information concerning medical care and procedures.
- The patient has a legal right to prompt attention, especially in an emergency situation.
- The patient has a legal right to a clear, concise explanation in layperson's terms of all proposed procedures, including the possibilities of any risk of mortality or serious side effects, problems related to recuperation, and probability of success, and will not be subjected to any procedure without his/her voluntary, competent and understanding consent. The specifics of such consent shall be set out in a written consent form, signed by the patient.
- The patient has a legal right to a clear, complete, and accurate evaluation of his/her condition and prognosis without treatment before being asked to consent to any test or procedure.
- We recognize the right of the patient to know the identity and professional status of all those providing service. All personnel have been instructed to introduce themselves, state their status, and explain their role in the health care of the patient. Part of this right is the right of the patient to know the identity of the physician responsible for his/her care.
- We recognize the right of any patient who does not speak English to have access to an interpreter.
- The patient has a right to all the information contained in his/her medical record while in the health-care facility, and to examine the record on request.
- We recognize the right of a patient to discuss his/her condition with a consultant specialist, at the patient's request and expense.
- The patient has a legal right not to have any test or procedure, designed for educational purposes rather than his/her direct personal benefit, performed on him/her.

- The patient has a legal right to refuse any particular drug, test, procedure, or treatment.
- The patient has a legal right to privacy of both person and information with respect to: the hospital staff, other doctors, residents, interns and medical students, researchers, nurses, other hospital personnel, and other patients.
- We recognize the patient's right of access to people outside the health-care facility by means of visitors and the telephone. Parents may stay with their children and relatives with terminally ill patients 24 hours a day.
- The patient has a legal right to leave the health-care facility regardless of his/her physical condition or financial status, although the patient may be requested to sign a release stating that he/she is leaving against the medical judgment of his/her doctor or the hospital.
- The patient has a right not to be transferred to another facility unless he/she has received a complete explanation of the desirability of and need for the transfer. If the patient does not agree to transfer, the patient has the right to a consultant's opinion on the desirability of transfer.
- A patient has a right to be notified of his/her impending discharge at least one day before it is accomplished, to insist on a consultation by an expert on the desirability of discharge, and to have a person of the patient's choice notified in advance.
- The patient has a right, regardless of the source of payment, to examine and receive an itemized and detailed explanation of the total bill for services rendered in the facility.
- The patient has a right to competent counseling from the hospital staff to help in obtaining financial assistance from public or private sources to meet the expense of services received in the institution.
- The patient has a right to timely prior notice of the termination of his/her eligibility for reimbursement by any third-party payor for the expense of hospital care.
- At the termination of his/her stay at the health-care facility

we recognize the right of a patient to a complete copy of the information contained in his/her medical record.

- We recognize the right of all patients to have 24-hour-a-day access to a patient's rights advocate, who may act on behalf of the patient to assert or protect the rights set out in this document.

D

American Nurses' Association Code for Nurses

The Code for Nurses is based upon belief about the nature of individuals, nursing, health, and society. Recipients and providers of nursing services are viewed as individuals and groups who possess basic rights and responsibilities, and whose values and circumstances command respect at all times. Nursing encompasses the promotion and restoration of health, the prevention of illness, and the alleviation of suffering. *The statements of the Code and their interpretation provide guidance for conduct and relationships in carrying out nursing responsibilities consistent with the ethical obligations of the profession and quality in nursing care.*

- The nurse provides services with respect for human dignity and the uniqueness of the client unrestricted by considerations of social or economic status, personal attributes, or the nature of health problems.
- The nurse safeguards the client's right to privacy by judiciously protecting information of a confidential nature.
- The nurse acts to safeguard the client and the public when health care and safety are affected by the incompetent, unethical, or illegal practice of any person.
- The nurse assumes responsibility and accountability for individual nursing judgments and actions.
- The nurse maintains competence in nursing.
- The nurse exercises informed judgment and uses individual competence and qualifications as criteria in seeking

consultation, accepting responsibilities, and delegating nursing activities to others.

- The nurse participates in activities that contribute to the ongoing development of the profession's body of knowledge.
- The nurse participates in the profession's efforts to implement and improve standards of nursing.
- The nurse participates in the profession's efforts to establish and maintain conditions of employment conducive to high-quality nursing care.
- The nurse participates in the profession's effort to protect the public from misinformation and misrepresentation and to maintain the integrity of nursing.
- The nurse collaborates with members of the health professions and other citizens in promoting community and national efforts to meet the health needs of the public.

E

Code of Ethics for the Licensed Practical Nurse

- The licensed practical nurse shall practice her profession with integrity.
- The licensed practical nurse shall be loyal—to the physician, to the patient, and to her employer.
- The licensed practical nurse strives to know her limitations and to stay within the bounds of these limitations.
- The licensed practical nurse is sincere in the performance of her duties and generous in rendering service.
- The licensed practical nurse considers no duty too menial if it contributes to the welfare and comfort of her patient.
- The licensed practical nurse accepts only that monetary compensation which is provided for in the contract under which she is employed, and she does not solicit gifts.
- The licensed practical nurse holds in confidence all information entrusted to her.
- The licensed practical nurse shall be a good citizen.
- The licensed practical nurse participates in and shares responsibility for meeting health needs.
- The licensed practical nurse faithfully carries out the orders of the physician or registered nurse under whom she serves.
- The licensed practical nurse refrains from entering into conversation with the patient about personal experiences, personal problems, and personal ailments.

- The licensed practical nurse abstains from administering self-medication, and in event of personal illness, takes only those medications prescribed by a licensed physician.
- The licensed practical nurse respects the dignity of the uniform by never wearing it in a public place.
- The licensed practical nurse respects the religious beliefs of all patients.
- The licensed practical nurse abides by the Golden Rule in her daily relationship with people in all walks of life.
- The licensed practical nurse is a member of The National Federation of Licensed Practical Nurses, Inc., and the state and local membership associations.
- The licensed practical nurse may give credit to a commercial product or service, but does not identify herself with advertising, sales, or, promotion.

F

International Council of Nurses Code for Nurses

The fundamental responsibility of the nurse is fourfold: to promote health, to prevent illness, to restore health, and to alleviate suffering.

The need for nursing is universal. Inherent in nursing is respect for life, dignity, and rights of man. It is unrestricted by considerations of nationality, race, creed, color, age, sex, politics, or social status.

Nurses render health services to the individual, the family, and the community, and coordinate their services with those of related groups.

Nurses and People

The nurse's primary responsibility is to those people who require nursing care.

The nurse, in providing care, respects the beliefs, values, and customs of the individual.

The nurse holds in confidence personal information and uses judgment in sharing this information.

Nurses and Practice

The nurse carries personal responsibility for nursing practice and for maintaining competence by continual learning.

The nurse maintains the highest standards of nursing care possible within the reality of a specific situation.

The nurse uses judgment in relation to individual competence when accepting and delegating responsibilities.

The nurse, when acting in a professional capacity, should at all times maintain standards of personal conduct that would reflect credit upon the profession.

Nurses and Society

The nurse shares with other citizens the responsibility for initiating and supporting action to meet the health and social needs of the public.

Nurses and Co-Workers

The nurse sustains a cooperative relationship with co-workers in nursing and other fields.

The nurse takes appropriate action to safeguard the individual when his care is endangered by a co-worker or any other person.

Nurses and the Profession

The nurse plays the major role in determining and implementing desirable standards of nursing practice and nursing education.

The nurse is active in developing a core of professional knowledge.

The nurse, acting through the professional organization, participates in establishing and maintaining equitable social and economic working conditions in nursing.

G

The American Nurses' Association's Standards of Nursing Practice

The American Nurses' Association developed the following standards of nursing practice in 1973 to give the courts, hospitals, nurses, and patients guidelines for determining quality nursing care. The standards are based on the steps of the nursing process: assessment, planning, implementation, and evaluation. Each standard is followed by a rationale—explaining the standard—and assessment factors for use in determining if the standard has been met.

STANDARD I

THE COLLECTION OF DATA ABOUT THE HEALTH STATUS OF THE CLIENT/PATIENT IS SYSTEMATIC AND CONTINUOUS. THE DATA ARE ACCESSIBLE, COMMUNICATED, AND RECORDED.

Rationale

Comprehensive care requires complete and ongoing collection of data about the client/patient to determine the nursing care needs of the client/patient. All health status data about the client/patient must be available for all members of the health-care team.

Assessment Factors

- Health status data include:
  —Growth and development
  —Biophysical status

—Emotional status
—Cultural, religious, socioeconomic background
—Performance of activities of daily living
—Patterns of coping
—Interaction patterns
—Client's/patient's perception of and satisfaction with his health status
—Client/patient health goals
—Environment (physical, social, emotional, ecological)
—Available and accessible human and material resources

- Data are collected from:
  —Client/patient, family, significant others
  —Health-care personnel
  —Individuals within the immediate environment and/or the community
- Data are obtained by:
  —Interview
  —Examination
  —Observation
  —Reading records, reports, etc.
- There is a format for the collection of data which:
  —Provides for a systematic collection of data
  —Facilitates the completeness of data collection
- Continuous collection of data is evident by:
  —Frequent updating
  —Recording of changes in health status
- The data are:
  —Accessible on the client/patient records
  —Retrievable from record-keeping systems
  —Confidential when appropriate

STANDARD II

NURSING DIAGNOSES ARE DERIVED FROM HEALTH STATUS DATA.

Rationale

The health status of the client/patient is the basis for determining the nursing care needs. The data are analyzed and compared to norms when possible.

Assessment Factors

- The client's/patient's health status is compared to the norm in order to determine if there is a deviation from the norm and the degree and direction of deviation.
- The client's/patient's capabilities and limitations are identified.
- The nursing diagnoses are related to and congruent with the diagnoses of all other professionals caring for the client/patient.

STANDARD III

THE PLAN OF NURSING CARE INCLUDES GOALS DERIVED FROM THE NURSING DIAGNOSES.

Rationale

The determination of the results to be achieved is an essential part of planning care.

Assessment Factors

- Goals are mutually set with the client/patient and pertinent others:
  —They are congruent with other planned therapies.
  —They are stated in realistic and measurable terms.
  —They are assigned a time period for achievement.
- Goals are established to maximize functional capabilities and are congruent with:
  —Growth and development
  —Biophysical status
  —Behavioral patterns
  —Human and material resources

STANDARD IV

THE PLAN OF NURSING CARE INCLUDES PRIORITIES AND THE PRESCRIBED NURSING APPROACHES OR MEASURES TO ACHIEVE THE GOALS DERIVED FROM THE NURSING DIAGNOSES.

Rationale

Nursing actions are planned to promote, maintain and restore the client's/patient's well-being.

Assessment Factors

- Physiological measures are planned to manage (prevent or control) specific patient problems and are related to the nursing diagnoses and goals of care, e.g., ADL, use of self-help devices, etc.
- Psychosocial measures are specific to the client's/patient's nursing care problem and to the nursing care goals, e.g., techniques to control aggression, motivation.
- Teaching-learning principles are incorporated into the plan of care and objectives for learning stated in behavioral terms, e.g., specification of content for learner's level, reinforcement, readiness, etc.
- Approaches are planned to provide for a therapeutic environment:
  —Physical environmental factors are used to influence the therapeutic environment, e.g., control of noise, control of temperature, etc.
  —Psychosocial measures are used to structure the environment for therapeutic ends, e.g., paternal participation in all phases of the maternity experience.
  —Group behaviors are used to structure interaction and influence the therapeutic environment, e.g., comformity, ethos, territorial rights, locomotion, etc.
- Approaches are specified for orientation of the client/patient to:
  —New roles and relationships
  —Relevant health (human and material) resources
  —Modifications in plan of nursing care
  —Relationship of modifications in nursing care plan to the total care plan
- The plan of nursing care includes the utilization of available and appropriate resources:
  —Human resources (other health personnel)
  —Material resources
  —Community
- The plan includes an ordered sequence of nursing actions
- Nursing approaches are planned on the basis of current scientific knowledge.

STANDARD V

NURSING ACTIONS PROVIDE FOR CLIENT/PATIENT PARTICIPATION IN HEALTH PROMOTION, MAINTENANCE AND RESTORATION.

Rationale

The client/patient and family are continually involved in nursing care.

Assessment Factors

- The client/patient and family are kept informed about:
  —Current health status
  —Changes in health status
  —Total health-care plan
  —Nursing care plan
  —Roles of health-care personnel
  —Health-care resources
- The client/patient and family are provided with the information needed to make decisions and choices about:
  —Promoting, maintaining and restoring health
  —Seeking and utilizing appropriate health-care personnel
  —Maintaining and using health-care resources

STANDARD VI

NURSING ACTIONS ASSIST THE CLIENT/PATIENT TO MAXIMIZE HIS HEALTH CAPABILITIES.

Rationale

Nursing actions are designed to promote, maintain and restore health.

Assessment Factors

- Nursing actions:
  —Are consistent with the plan of care.
  —Are based on scientific principles.
  —Are individualized to the specific situation.
  —Are used to provide a safe and therapeutic environment.
  —Employ teaching-learning opportunities for the client/patient.
  —Include utilization of appropriate resources.

- Nursing actions are directed by the client's/patient's physical, physiological, psychological and social behavior associated with:
  —Ingestion of food, fluid and nutrients
  —Elimination of body wastes and excesses in fluid
  —Locomotion and exercise
  —Regulatory mechanisms—body heat, metabolism
  —Relating to others
  —Self-actualization

STANDARD VII

THE CLIENT'S/PATIENT'S PROGRESS OR LACK OF PROGRESS TOWARD GOAL ACHIEVEMENT IS DETERMINED BY THE CLIENT/PATIENT AND THE NURSE.

Rationale

The quality of nursing care depends upon comprehensive and intelligent determination of nursing's impact upon the health status of the client/patient. The client/patient is an essential part of this determination.

Assessment Factors

- Current data about the client/patient are used to measure his progress toward goal achievement.
- Nursing actions are analyzed for their effectiveness in the goal achievement of the client/patient.
- The client/patient evaluates nursing actions and goal achievement.
- Provision is made for nursing follow-up of a particular client/patient to determine the long-term effects of nursing care.

STANDARD VIII

THE CLIENT'S/PATIENT'S PROGRESS OR LACK OF PROGRESS TOWARD GOAL ACHIEVEMENT DIRECTS REASSESSMENT, REORDERING OF PRIORITIES, NEW GOAL SETTING AND REVISION OF THE PLAN OF NURSING CARE.

Rationale

The nursing process remains the same, but the input of new information may dictate new or revised approaches.

Assessment Factors

- Reassessment is directed by goal achievement or lack of goal achievement.
- New priorities and goals are determined and additional nursing approaches are prescribed appropriately.
- New nursing actions are accurately and appropriately initiated.

Legal Glossary

Accomplice: A person who knowingly, voluntarily, and with common intent with the main offender helps in a crime. "Accomplice" includes all persons connected with the offense by an unlawful act or omission either before, at the time of, or after the commission of the offense, whether this witness was present or participated in the crime or not.

Action: The legal demand of one's right from another person or party made in a court of justice.

Admission: A statement against his or her interest made by a party to an action.

Affidavit: A written statement or declaration under oath.

Amicus Curiae: "A friend of the court." An outsider (usually an attorney) who voluntarily appears to file a brief (as *amicus curiae*) and offers information on some matter of law where the judge is doubtful or mistaken, or on a matter of which the court may take judicial recognition.

Appeal: A petition to a superior court to review and correct or reverse a possible error committed by a lower court, whose judgment or decision the court appeals is called upon to correct or reverse.

Arbitration: The investigation and determination of a matter of difference between parties by one or more unofficial persons chosen by the parties. These are called arbitrators, referees or mediators.

Argument: An effort to establish facts by a course of reasoning. For example, the speech of counsel to persuade a jury.

Attachment: A proceeding—to take a defendant's property

into legal custody to satisfy a plaintiff's legal demand. The object is to hold the property to obey the order of the court for the payment of a judgment in case a defendant must make payment on the debt.

Case: A general term for an action, cause, suit, or controversy, at law or in equity. *Case at bar* refers to the particular case that is before the court.

Prima facie case: A case established by having enough evidence. This case can be overthrown only by denying evidence cited by the other side. (See *rebut*.)

Cause: Any question, civil or criminal, challenged before a court of justice.

Common Law: The common law is that body of law and juristic theory that was originated, developed, and formulated, and is administered, in England, and has been the law among most of the states.

Complaint: The complaint is the first or initiatory pleading on the part of the plaintiff in a civil action. It corresponds to the declaration in the common-law practice.

Cross-complaint: Whenever the defendant seeks affirmative relief against any party, relating to the transaction upon which the action is brought, he may, in addition to his answer, file a cross-complaint. Both complaint and cross-complaint contain a statement of the facts, and each demands relief on the facts stated. Each is served upon the opposite party, and each must be answered or other legal pleading must be taken if default judgment is to be avoided.

Answer: The formal, written statement under code state provisions, made by a defendant presenting the grounds of his or her defense. It corresponds to what in actions under the common-law practice is called the "plea"; however, as used in a statute providing that the defendant must appear and answer the petition (or declaration), "answer" refers to any pleading filed by the defendant.

Compromise: An arrangement arrived at, either in court or out of court, for settling an argument on what appears to both parties to be equitable terms. Proof of an offer to compromise the controversy involved in litigation, or the fact that an offer to compromise was made, is held not to be permitted as evidence.

Conspiracy: A confederacy between two or more persons formed for the purpose of committing, by their joint efforts, some unlawful act or for the purpose of using unlawful means for the commission of an act lawful in itself.

Contempt: A willful disregard or disobedience of the court's orders, as well as such conduct that tends to bring the authority of the court and the administration of justice into question.

Contract: An agreement, to do or not to do a certain thing.

Express contract: An actual agreement of the parties, the terms of which are openly declared at the time of making it, stated in distinct and explicit language either orally or in writing.

Implied contract: A contract not created or evidenced by the explicit agreement of the parties but implied by law, as a matter of reason and justice from their acts of conduct, the circumstances surrounding the transaction making it a reasonable or even a necessary assumption that a contract existed between them by clear understanding.

Contribution: The sharing of a loss or payment; a payment made by each or any of several, having a common interest of liability, or his or her share in the loss suffered or money necessarily paid by one in behalf of others.

Count: In pleading, the different parts of a declaration or complaint, each of which, if it stood alone, would be a ground for action. *Count* is also used to signify the several parts of an indictment, each charging a distinct offense.

Court: The judicial department of the government whose function is the application of the laws to controversies brought before it and the public administration of justice.

Covenant Not to Sue: An agreement by one who at the time of making it had a right of action against another person, but who agreed not to sue to enforce such right of action.

Deposition: Specifically applied to the testimony of a witness taken in writing, under oath or affirmation, before some judicial officer in answer to oral or written questions.

Directed Verdict: When there is not enough evidence or cause resulting from the evidence which would support a judgment for the one party, the court may, on motion of the other party, direct the jury to bring in a verdict for that other party. (See *verdict*.)

Due Care: Due or ordinary care means the degree of care that would be exercised by the ordinary careful person in the same circumstances.

Equity: Equity is a system administered by a tribunal, other than the established courts, developed because of the inability or the unwillingness of the common law to meet all the requirements of justice. Courts of equity have been called courts of conscience because their object is to deal with legal controversies to allow for full, adequate, and complete justice between the parties in accordance with the dictates of natural justice and good conscience.

Error: An error of the court in applying the law to the case on trial. For example, in ruling on the admissibility of evidence or in charging (instructing) the jury.

Estoppel: A bar or barrier raised by the law that prevents a person from stating or denying a certain fact or state of facts in consequence of his or her previous statements or denial of conduct or admission, or the result of a final judgment of the matter in a court of law; a person's act or acceptance that stops or closes his or her mouth to state or prove the truth.

Ethics: The branch of moral science that deals with the duties a member of a profession owes to the public, to his or her colleagues, and to his or her patients or clients.

Evidence: Proof or test of a matter legally presented at the trial of an issue by the parties involved by using witnesses, records, documents, concrete objects, and so forth to influence the minds of the court or jury about their opposition.

Direct evidence: When the existence of any fact is proven by witnesses as having come under the awareness of their own senses, or is stated in documents, the genuineness and truth of which there seems no reason to question, the evidence of that fact is said to be direct.

Circumstantial evidence: Evidence that suggestively proves the principle fact by establishing a condition of surrounding and limiting circumstances; the existence of the principle fact is only decided by one or more circumstances that have been established directly.

Execution: A judicial writ issued by the court when the judgment is made, directed to an officer of the court, and running against the body or goods of a party, by which the judgment of the court is enforced. In general, execution may be issued against any party against whom a judgment may be made. Every kind of property or interest not otherwise exempt by statute may be reached by an execution issued on a judgment.

Ex Parte: An *ex parte* proceeding is a proceeding by and for one party only, without notice to or opposition by another.

Felony: A crime of a more serious nature than those known as misdemeanors. In many states felony is defined as any public offense on conviction of which the offender is liable to sentence of death or imprisonment in a penitentiary or state prison; in contrast, misdemeanor is a general name for criminal offenses that do not in law amount to the grade of felony.

Fraud: A standard term that covers the numerous means that can be thought of by the human mind, and carried out by one individual, to gain an advantage over another by false statement or by hiding the truth.

Garnishment: A legal summons or attachment of property to satisfy a debt. Also, the withholding of a certain sum from wages to satisfy a creditor.

Grand Jury: A jury that looks at accusations against parties charged with crimes, and if the evidence warrants, the jury makes formal charges on which the accused parties are later tried.

Hearsay Evidence: Evidence not gained from the personal

knowledge of a witness but from what the witness has heard other parties say.

Indemnify: The process of repaying a party for losses brought on when the obligation to repay under a contractual provision exists.

Indemnity: A contract where one person attempts to protect another person against an anticipated loss.

Independent Contractor: A person who contracts with another to do something for him or her. This person is not controlled by the other or subject to the other's right to control with respect to his or her physical conduct in the performance of the task.

Indictment: An accusation in writing created by a legally summoned and sworn grand jury presented by this jury to the court which it is enrolled in, charging that a person named in the accusation has done some act or been guilty of some omission which, by law, is a public offense punishable on indictment.

Inference: A conclusion reached by the jury from the facts proven.

Information: An accusation in the nature of an indictment. It is different from an indictment by being presented by a competent public officer on his or her oath of office instead of by a grand jury on their oath.

Injunction: A legal action by a court of equity forbidding a party from carrying out a certain action.

Instruction by the Court: An explanation of the rules or principles of law applicable to some case, which the jury is bound to accept and apply.

Insurance: A contract by which one party assumes certain risks of another party, and promises to pay the party or his or her nominee a certain or proven sum of money under special circumstances.

Invasion of Privacy: Interfering on the right of privacy, or the right to be "left alone," to live alone without being subjected to unwarranted or unwanted publicity.

Issue: A single and material point resulting from the allegations of the parties.

Judgment: The decision or sentence of the law given by a court resulting from the proceedings of the court.

Judgment by default: Judgment taken against a defendant when, having been summoned or cited in an action, he fails to appear at the proper time. In cases where a motion for a directed verdict should have been granted but was denied, the court on its own motion or on the motion of the aggrieved party may pass judgment without the verdict of the jury.

Jury: A certain number of persons, selected by law, who are sworn to look into certain matters of fact and to declare the truth upon evidence presented before them.

Justice: To give every person his due.

Legal Duty: An obligation resulting from contract of the parties or the operation of the law.

Liability: The state of being bound or obliged in law or justice to do, pay, or make good on something. A legal liability is one where courts of justice recognize and enforce, such as that between opposing parties.

Malfeasance: The wrongful or unjust performance of some act that the performer has no right to perform, or that he or she is demanded by contract not to do.

Misfeasance. The improper performance of some act that a person may lawfully do.

Nonfeasance. The neglect or failure of a person to do some act that he or she should do.

Mandamus (Latin, *we command*): A writ issued by a superior court demanding that a certain act or duty be carried out by a governmental body or officer.

Mens Rea: A guilty mind; a guilty or wrongful purpose; a criminal intent.

Moral Turpitude: An act of dishonesty, evil, or corruption in the private and social duties that a man owes to his fellow men or to society in general. However, such acts are not immoral in themselves but their illegality lies in the fact of their being positively forbidden by law.

Negligence: The omission to do something that a reasonable person, guided by those ordinary considerations that commonly regulate human affairs, would do, or the doing of something that a reasonable and prudent person would not do.

Nonsuit: A judgment against the plaintiff when he is unable to prove a case, or when he refuses or neglects to proceed to the trial of a cause after it has been put in issue. Only a defendant may move for a nonsuit. The directed verdict is a bar to another action but a nonsuit is not.

Perjury: Willfully giving, under oath, false testimony important to the issue or point of inquiry in a judicial proceeding or course of justice.

Police Power: The natural power of a government to have reasonable control over people and property in the interest of the general security, health, safety, morals, and welfare.

Precedent: A ruled case or court decision used to furnish an example or authority for an identical or similar case afterward raising a similar question of law.

Preponderance of Evidence: Evidence of greater weight or more convincing than the evidence offered in opposition to it.

Presumption: A deduction that the law expressly directs be made from certain facts.

Privileged Communication: A communication between parties to a confidential relation so that the receiver cannot be legally forced to reveal it as a witness. For example, a communication between attorney and client, husband and wife, physician and patient, and so forth.

Privity: Mutual or successive relationship to the same rights of property.

Probative: Having the effect of proof; tending to prove or actually proving. (See *proof.*).

Proof: The establishment of a fact by evidence.

Public Policy: The principle of law that holds that no subject can lawfully do something that may be injurious to the public or against the public good.

Rebut: To rebut is to defeat or take away from the action of something. For example, when a plaintiff in an action produces evidence that raises the possibility of the defendant's liability, and the defendant shows evidence that shows that the presumption is ill-founded, he or she is said to "rebut it."

Release: A written contract for which some claim or interest in something is surrendered to another person.

Remand: To remand a case brought into an appellate court, or a case removed from one court into another, means to send it back to the court from which it came so that further proceedings in the case, if any, may be taken there.

Res Ipso Loquitor: "The thing speaks for itself." Apparent negligence of common knowledge.

Res Judicata: A matter decided; a thing judicially acted upon or decided.

Respectable Minority Rule: Where there is more than one recognized and approved method of treatment applicable to a case, the physician or surgeon is not liable for honest mistakes of judgment in selecting a method. A charge of negligence in a choice of treatment is denied by showing that a respectable minority of expert physicians approved the method selected.

Respondeat Superior: "Let the master answer." This saying means that a master is liable in certain cases for the wrongful acts of his or her servants and is a principal for those of his or her agent.

Right: That which a person in entitled to have, or to do, or to receive from others within the limits of the law.

Slander: Oral defamation; speaking false words about another resulting in injury to his or her reputation.

Stare Decisis: The principle that the laws we are governed by should be fixed and known. When the law is declared by a court of jurisdiction competent to interpret it, such a declaration is itself evidence of the law until it is changed by competent authority.

Stipulation: The term normally given to an agreement made by the attorneys engaged on opposite sides of a cause.

Subpoena: A writ or order directed to a person requiring his or her attendance at a particular time and place to testify. It may also require the person to bring any books, documents, or other things under his or her control that he or she is bound by law to produce as evidence (*subpoena duces tecum*).

Summons: A writ directed to the sheriff or other proper officer requiring him to notify the person named that an action has been started against him and that he is required to appear on a day named to answer the complaint in such action.

Surety: A person who contracts himself for the payment of a sum of money, or for the performance for another person; a person who, being liable to pay a debt or perform an obligation, is entitled, if it is enforced against him or her, to be repaid by some other person who should have made payment or performed before the surety was compelled to do so.

Tort: A legal wrong committed on the person or property of another independent of a contract for which the law gives a civil remedy.

Tort-Feasor: One who commits or is guilty of a tort. To be "joint tort-feasors," the parties must either act together in committing the wrong, or their acts, if independent of each other, must unite in causing a single injury.

Verdict: The final answer given by the jury to the court concerning the matters of fact committed to the jury for their deliberation and determination. (See *directed verdict*.)

Will: A written instrument, executed with the formalities of law, whereby a person makes disposition of his property after his death.

Writ: A notice or order, usually issued by a court.

Index